THE TRAGEDIES
OF THE MEDICI

BIANCA CAPPELLO-BUONAVENTURI.

THE TRAGEDIES OF THE MEDICI

BY EDGCUMBE STALEY

AUTHOR OF "THE GUILDS OF FLORENCE,"
"RAPHAEL," "FRA ANGELICO," ETC.

ILLUSTRATED

NEW YORK
BRENTANO'S
PUBLISHERS

TO THE MEMORY OF MY
FATHER
THOMAS STALEY

Printed by Fox, Jones & Co., Kemp Hall Press, Oxford, England

PREFACE

WHEN Alexandre Dumas wrote his *Crimes of the Borgias*
—and other "Crimes"—he fully intended to compile
a companion volume, treating of episodes in the great
family of the Medici. With this project in view, he
collected much material, and actually published, tenta-
tively, two interesting brochures : *Une Année a Florence*
—in 1841, and *Les Galeries de Florence*—in 1842.

Nothing, however, came of his more ambitious "idea,"
and, until to-day, no one has taken in hand to write
The Tragedies of the Medici. My attention was first
directed to the omission during the preparation of my
Guilds of Florence, published in 1906 ; and I determined
to address myself to the forging of that lurid link in the
catena of Florentine romance.

In the following pages my readers will see that I
have entirely departed from the conventional conceits
of the ordinary historian. I have sought to set out the
whole truth—not a garbled version—whilst I have
fearlessly added decorative features where facts were
absent or were too prosaic.

The short "Introduction," dealing with the rise
and progress of the house of Medici, will be useful to
my public, and the "Chart of the Tragedies" will assist
students and others in their appreciation of my enterprise—it is my own compilation and as complete as
possible.

The "Bibliography" will help serious readers to a
wider reading of my authorities, and the Illustrations—
the best procurable—will fix in all my readers' minds
something of the actual personalities of my "Tyrants"
and my "Victims."

EDGCUMBE STALEY.

CONTENTS

LIST OF ILLUSTRATIONS

INTRODUCTION

THE origin of the Medici family is lost in the mists of the Middle Ages, and, only here and there, can the historian gain glimpses of the lives of early forbears. Still, there is sufficient data, to be had for the digging, upon which to transcribe, inferentially at least, an interesting narrative.

Away towards the end of the twelfth century,—exact dates are wholly beside the mark—there dwelt, under the shadow of one of the rugged castles of the robber-captains of the Mugello in Tuscany, a hard-working and trustworthy bondsman—one Chiarissimo—" Old Honesty," as we may call him. He was married to an excellent helpmeet, and was by his lord permitted to till a small piece of land and rear his family.

In addition to intelligence in agriculture, it would seem that he, or perhaps his wife, possessed some knowledge of the virtues of roots and herbs, for, in one corner of his *podere*, he had a garden of " simples." The few peaceable inhabitants of that warlike valley, and also many a wounded man-at-arms, sought " Old Honesty " and his wise mate for what we now call " kitchen remedies."

Those, indeed, were happy days with respect to suffering human nature. " Kill or Cure " might have been the character of the healing art, but certainly specialists had not invented our appendicitis and other fashionable twentieth-century physical fashions ! A little medical knowledge sufficed, and decoctions, pillules, poultices, and bleedings made up the simple pharmacopœia.

All the same, the satirical rhyme, which an old

chronicler put into the mouths of many a despairing patient, in later days, may have been true also of " Old Honesty " and his nostrums :

> " There's not a herb nor a root
> Nor any remedy to boot
> Which can stave death off by a foot ! "

Of that good couple's family only one name has been preserved—Gianbuono, " Good John." Passerini says he was a priest—probably he means a hermit. Anyhow, he acquired more property in the Valle della Sieve and founded a church—Santa Maria dell' Assunta—possibly the enlargement of his cell—upon Monte Senario, between the valley of the Arno and that of the Sieve.

Ser Gianbuono—ecclesiastic or not—had two sons— Bonagiunto, " Lucky Lad," and Chiarissimo II. In those primitive times nobody troubled about surnames— idiosyncrasy of any kind was a sufficient indication of individuality. The brothers were enterprising fellows, and both made tracks for Florence, which—risen Phoenix-like from barbarian ashes—was thriving marvellously as a mart for art and craft.

Ser Bonagiunto, in the first decade of the thirteenth century, was living in the Sestiere di Porta del Duomo, and working busily in wood and stone, the stalwart parent of a vigorous progeny. It was his great-grandson, Ardingo—a famous athlete in the *giostre* and a soldier of renown—who first of his family attained the rank of *Signore*.

Ser Chiarissimo, between 1201–1210, owned a tower near San Tommaso, at the north-east angle of the Mercato Vecchio—later, the family church of the Medici—and under it a *bottega*, or *canova*, for the sale of his grandmother's recipes. Over the door he put up

Introduction

his sign—seven golden *Pillole di Speziale*—pills or balls, which were emblazoned upon the proud escutcheon of his descendants. He was called "*il Medico*"—"the doctor"—hence the family name "Medici."

These were the days when the foundations of the fortunes of many great Florentine families were laid. The loaning of money was the royal road to affluence, and everybody who, by chance, had a spare gold florin, or two, became *ipso facto* a "*Presto*" or bank. Next, after lending to one another with a moderate profit—a *dono di tempo* or a *merito*—"quick returns," came the ambitious system of State loans, with the regulated *interesso* and the speculative dealings in *Cambio*—on 'Change—with *boroccolo*—"unexpected gain," and *ritravgola*—"sly advantage," or, as we say, "sharp practice."

Ser Filippo, or "Lippo"—the twin son, as the name implies, of Ser Chiarissimo II.—what happened to the other twin we do not know—was probably the first of his family of doctor-apothecaries to deliberately abandon his less lucrative profession and establish himself as a banker in the Mercato Nuovo. Anyhow, his two sons were born and baptised under the happy auspices of plenty of money !

The elder, the prosperous doctor-banker, was jubilantly called Averardo—"Blessed with good means," and the younger was christened Chiarissimo III., to mark quite sententiously that, whilst his bank-balance was considerable, it had been accumulated by honest dealing !

True to the variable law of vicissitude, this Averardo I. failed to make any very great name for himself, as might have been expected in a lad of so much promise. He was shadowed doubtless by his more strenuous parent. Still, he added to the family possessions by

Introduction

acquiring the lay-patronage of the churches of San Pietro a Sieve and San Bartolommeo di Petrone. Near the latter he built a *castello*, or fortress, which was then considered a title to nobility. He made also a prosperous marriage with Donna Benricevuta de' Sizi.

Messer Averardo's son, Averardo II., was, in the crisscross nature of things, a man of stronger grit than his father. He came to great honour as well as to great riches. Elected Prior in 1304, he was chosen as *Gonfaloniere di Giustizia* in 1314, and, between these dates, in 1311, Ser Teghia de' Sizi, his mother's brother, made him his heir, and gave him, besides full money-bags, much valuable property and ecclesiastical patronage. To his surname of Medici he added that of Sizi : he was the wealthiest citizen of his day in Florence. His wife, Donna Mandina di Filippo de' Arrigucci of Fiesole, gave him six sons—Giacopo, Giovenco, Francesco, Salvestro, Talento, and Conte. All of them rose to eminence in the State, but of one only can the story be told here—Salvestro.

Messer Salvestro de' Medici—who must not be confounded with his celebrated namesake and kinsman, the " Grand " Salvestro—married Donna Lisa de' Donati, of which union three sons were the issue—Talento, Giovenco, and Averardo III. Salvestro di Averardo II. bore another Christian name—Chiarissimo—the old-world cognomen of his family. Possibly his father thought it wise to stand well with the world and parade his honesty ; for whatever ill-gotten gains other bankers acquired, he, at least, was an upright man, and his profits were just !

Anyhow, Messer Salvestro became popular for rectitude in his private life, and for his unselfish discharge of public duties. He was chosen to fill many responsible offices of State, and reached the goal of personal ambition

Introduction

as ambassador to Venice, in 1336. His youngest son, Averardo III., acquired the sobriquet of " Bicci "—the exact meaning of which is problematical—it may mean a " worthless fellow " or " one who lives in a castle ! " Nothing indeed is related of him, but, perhaps, like Brer Fox, of a later epoch, he was content " to lie low " and enjoy, without much exertion, the good things his ancestors had provided for him.

Messer Averardo married twice—Giovanna de' Cavallini and Giovanna de' Spini. By the first he became the father of one of the very greatest of the Medici—Giovanni, the parent of a still more famous son —Cosimo.

At this period Florence was ruled by Whalter von Brienne—the so-called Duke of Athens—sagacious, treacherous and depraved. He sought to make himself Lord of Florence by skilfully playing the various political parties one against the other. The *Grandi* he kept in check by the *Popolo Minuto*, but ignored the *Popolo Grasso*, to which the Medici belonged. Under Giovanni de' Medici, Guglielmo degli Altoviti, and Bernardo de' Rucellai, the middle class rose against the usurper ; but their plans miscarried, and the leaders were imprisoned and fined.

A Giovanni de' Medici was beheaded in 1342—the first recorded " Tragedy of the Medici." As to who this unfortunate man was, it is difficult to say. He is called " the son of Bernardo de' Medici," but no such name appears in the early records of the family. He was probably a descendant of Bonagiunto, a son of Ardingo de' Medici, who was a violent enemy of the Ghibellines, and *Gonfaloniere di Giustizia*, in 1296 and 1307, and brother of Francesco, Captain of Pistoja in 1338, and one of the principal participants in the expulsion of the hated Duke.

Introduction

The first of the " Grand " Medici was Salvestro, son of Alamanno, of the line of Chiarissimo III., called " The German," because of his alien Teutonic mother. Great-great-grandson of Ser Filippo, the last of the doctor-apothecaries, Salvestro does not appear to have gone in for the steady, unromantic life of a banker, but to have addressed his energies to the profession of arms. Nevertheless, he was chosen Prior in 1318, and contributed, during peace, to the advancement of his city's interest. Upon the outbreak of war with the Visconti of Milan, in 1351, he was appointed commander of the Florentine forces.

His sterling grit made itself apparent in the vigour with which at the head of no more than one hundred men he relieved the town and fortress of Scarperia, on the Mugello hills, besieged by the invaders. For his bravery he was knighted by the *Signoria*. Cavaliere Salvestro de' Medici sided with the aristocratic party, and proclaimed himself a Ghibelline—consorting with the noble families of Albizzi, Ricci, and Strozzi. Their aim was to convert the Republic into an oligarchy under Piero degli Albizzi.

The *Popolo Minuto*, thoroughly alarmed at this menace of liberty and popular government, appointed leaders, who approached Cavaliere Salvestro, in 1370, when he held the supreme office of *Gonfaloniere di Giustizia*, to safeguard the interests of the tradespeople and lower classes. He gave heed to their representations, for he cunningly perceived that he might ride into the undisputed leadership of the great popular party, the Guelphs, and so checkmate his other allies, the aristocrats ! As head of a powerful branch of the rising family of Medici, members of the *Popolo Grasso*, or wealthy middle class, Cavaliere Salvestro became the champion of the people. All round his popularity was established

Introduction

for people said, " He was born for the safety of the Republic." He was tactful enough to conceal the personal bent of his policy, and acted upon the maxim, which he was never tired of repeating : " Never make a show before the people ! " As *Gonfaloniere* he summoned a Parliament of representatives of all parties and classes at the Palazzo Vecchio, with a view to the composition of differences and the maintenance of public order.

The Ghibellines would have none of his proposals, but privately they were divided amongst themselves, seeing which, the Cavaliere astutely announced the resignation of his office. This had the effect he expected —the Palazzo and the Piazza outside rang with the old cry—" *Liberta !* " " *Liberta !* " " *Evviva il Popolo !* " " *Evviva il Gonfaloniere !* " Salvestro de' Medici was master of the situation—the first of his family to attain the virtual, if not the real, control of the State.

The revolution spread through the city ; the palaces of the Ghibelline nobles were sacked and burnt. A period of discord and disaster followed, but, with the firm hand of Salvestro de' Medici upon the helm of the ship of the Republic, matters settled. In 1376 he was unanimously chosen *Capitano della Parte Guelfa*—an office of still more personal influence than the Gonfaloniership. No one questioned his authority. He was, as the historian, Michaele Bruto, has recorded, " The first of his family to show his successors how that by conciliating the middle and lower classes they could make their way to sovereignty."

Another crisis in the history of Florence arose in 1378, during Cavaliere Salvestro de' Medici's second Gonfaloniership, when the *Ciompi*—" Wooden Shoes " they were called in derision—the wool-workers—rose *en masse*, and besieged the *Signoria* sitting at the Palazzo

Vecchio. They claimed to rule the city and to abolish the nobles, and a second time Salvestro was " the man of the hour ! "

Acting upon his advice, terms were arranged with the revolutionaries, and Michaele Lando—a common woolcarder by trade, but a born leader of men—was elected *Gonfaloniere di Giustizia*, and a new government was set up. Upon Salvestro, " the Champion of the People," was again conferred by public acclamation the accolade of knighthood ; moreover, as a further mark of popular estimation, to him were allocated the rents of the shops upon the Ponte Vecchio and other prerogatives.

The public spirit displayed by Cavaliere Salvestro gained for him not only personal distinction and reward, but obtained for his family recognition as the first in Florence. He married Donna Bartolommea, the daughter of Messer Oddo degli Altoviti, by whom he had many children. None of his sons seem to have added laurels to the family fame, but to have lived peacefully in the glamour of their father's renown. The Cavaliere retired into private life in 1380, and his death, which occurred in 1388, marked the establishment of Medicean domination in the affairs of Florence.

The second of the " Grand " Medici was Giovanni, the son of Averardo III.—called " Bicci "—and his first wife, Donna Giovanna de' Cavallini, born in 1360. He was just twenty-eight years of age when his popular relative, Cavaliere Salvestro de' Medici, died. His young manhood found him in the very forefront of party strife, and from the first he held unswervingly with the Guelphs.

Married, in 1384, to Donna Piccarda, daughter of Messer Odoardo de' Bueri, he was the father of four sons—Antonio, Damiano, Cosimo, and Lorenzo—the two former died in childhood. The choice of names for

GIOVANNI D'AVERARDO DE' MEDICI — called "Bicci."
Angelo Bronzino.

UFFIZI GALLERY, FLORENCE

Introduction

two of the boys is significant of the value Messer Giovanni placed upon his family's origin—Saints Damiano and Cosimo, of course, were patrons of doctors and apothecaries. Hence he was not ashamed of the golden pillules of his armorial bearings !

Messer Giovanni developed extraordinary strength of character ; he was a born ruler of men, and a passionate patriot. He gained the goodwill of his fellow-citizens by his unselfishness and generosity—truly not too common in the bearing of men of his time. He served the office of Prior in 1402, 1408, 1411 ; he was ambassador to Naples in 1406, and to Pope Alessandro V. in 1409 ; and, in 1407, he held the lucrative post of Podesta of Pistoja.

In 1421 Messer Giovanni de' Medici was elected *Gonfaloniere di Giustizia*, as the representative of the middle classes, and in opposition to Messeri Rinaldo degli Albizzi and Niccolo da Uzzano, the Ghibelline nominees. The Republic sighed for peace, the crafts for quietness ; but the immense liabilities incurred by many costly military enterprises had to be met. Messer Giovanni proposed, in 1427, a tax which should not weigh too heavily upon anybody. Each citizen who was possessed of a capital of one hundred gold florins, or more, was mulcted in a payment to the State of half a gold florin (ten shillings *circa*). This tax, which was called " *Il Catasto*," was unanimously accepted—" it pleased the common people greatly." Messer Giovanni was taxed as heavily as anyone, namely, three hundred gold florins—indicative, incidentally, of his wealth and honesty.

Giovanni associated with himself another prominent man, Messer Agnolo de' Pandolfini, the leader of the " Peace-at-any-Price " party, who is remembered in the annals of Florence as " The Peaceful Citizen." The

Introduction

main points of their policy were :—(1) Peace abroad ;
(2) Prosperity at home ; (3) Low taxation.

No combination of his opponents—and they were
many and unscrupulous—was able to damage Messer
Giovanni's reputation and power. He could, had he
wished it, have proclaimed himself sole ruler of Florence
and her territory ; but self-control and prudence—
which were so characteristic of the men of his family—
never forsook him. He died universally regretted in
1429, and was buried in the church of San Lorenzo,
which he, along with the Martelli, had restored and
endowed.

Giovanni di Averardo de' Medici was looked upon as
the first banker in Italy, the controller of the credit of
Florence and the prince of financiers. Calvalcanti,
Macchiavelli, Ammirato, and almost all other historians,
describe him as " Large-hearted, liberal-minded,
courteous and charitable, dispensing munificent alms
with delicate consideration of the feelings and wants of
those whom he assisted. Never suing for honours,
he gained them all. Hostile to public peculations he
strove disinterestedly for the public good. He died
rich in this world's goods, but richer still in the goodwill
of his fellow-citizens."

Many have sought, nevertheless, to belittle Messer
Giovanni's reputation—attributing to him a motive for
all his urbanity—that of the permanent domination of
his house in the government of the Republic—not surely
a fault. His old rival in the arena of politics, Niccolo
da Uzzano, ever spoke of him after his death with
unstinted praise and admiration.

Messer Giovanni shares with Cavaliere Salvestro the
undying fame of having raised, upon the excellent
foundation laid by their ancestors, the massive support-
ing walls of that superb edifice, of which his son, Cosimo,

Introduction

formed the cupola, and his great-grandson, Lorenzo—the lantern—" the Light of Italy."

The third and fourth "Grand" Medici were, of course, Cosimo, "*Il Padre della Patria*," and Lorenzo, "*Il Magnifico*." The stories of their lives and exploits are to be read in the stories, the literature and the arts of Florence. Of Cosimo, Niccolo Macchiavelli wrote as follows :

" He applied himself so strenuously to increase the political power of his house, that those who had rejoiced at Giovanni's death now regretted it, perceiving what manner of man Cosimo was. Of consummate prudence, staid yet agreeable presence, he was liberal and humane. He never worked against his own party, or against the State, and was prompt in giving aid to all. His liberality gained him many partisans among the citizens."

Born in 1389, he early evinced mercantile proclivities, and when a lad of no more than seventeen Messer Giovanni, his father, placed him in charge successively of several of the foreign agencies of the Medici bank. Young Cosimo used his opportunities so well that he was looked upon as a successful financier, and came to be called " The Great Merchant of Florence ! "

He was jokingly wont to say : " Two yards of scarlet cloth are enough to make a citizen ! " Nevertheless he had a deep regard for the opinions and privileges of his fellow Florentines. One of his constant sayings was : " One must always consult the will of the people "—and " the people " replied by acclaiming him " *Il Padre della Patria*."

Cosimo has been called " a great merchant and a grand party-leader : the first of Florentines by birth and the first of Italians by culture." He died in 1464. His father left in cash a fortune of nearly 180,000 gold florins, but Cosimo's estate totalled upwards of 230,000 —*circa* £100,000—a vast amount in those days !

Introduction

After the strong personality of Cosimo and his masterful manipulation of commercial and political affairs, perhaps the unambitious rule of his son Piero was a necessary and healthful corollary. Piero de' Medici maintained the ground his father had made his own, and gave away nothing of the predominance of his family, and he made way, after a brief exercise of authority, for his brilliant son, Lorenzo.

Piero's character and career again prove the truth of the adage : " Ability rarely runs in two successive generations." All the same, he died in 1469, leaving his sons the heirs to nearly 300,000 gold florins !

Lorenzo, "*Il Magnifico*," was the first of the " Grand " Medici to give up entirely all connection with commercial pursuits and banking interests. His tenure of office, by a curious paradox, marks the termination of the financial liberties of Florence ! He was an all-round genius—there was nothing he could not do—and do well ! " Whatever is worth doing at all," he was wont to say, " is worth doing well."

With his death, in 1492, as Benedetto Dei said, "The Splendour, not of Tuscany only, but of all Italy, disappeared."

With the beginning of the sixteenth century dawned a new era. Preliminary signs had appeared in the growth of wealth, in enfranchisement from primitive methods, and in the evolution of individualism. Love of country and the ties of family life were loosened by the universal craving for self-indulgence and personal distinction. Idleness, sensuality, and scepticism—three baneful sisters—gained the mastery, weakening the fabric of society, and leading on to the evil courses of tyrannicide.

" The gradual extinction of public spirit ; the general deterioration of private character, and the exercise of

Introduction

unbridled lust and passion, are the livid hues which tinge with the purple of melancholy and the scarlet of tragedy the later pages of Florentine story."

.   .   .   .

The direct line of Cosimo, " *Il Padre della Patria*," the elder surviving son of Messer Giovanni di Averardo " Bicci" de' Medici, ended with Caterina, Queen of France, the only legitimate child of Lorenzo, Duke of Urbino, and last *Capo della Repubblica* of Florence ; and Alessandro the Bastard, first Duke of Florence, illegitimate son of Pope Clement VII.

The Sovereignty of the Medici was maintained in the person of Cosimo, the only son of Condottiere Giovanni, " delle Bande Nere," the great-grandson of Lorenzo, the younger of the two surviving sons of Messer Giovanni di Averardo " Bicci " de' Medici. The rule of the Medici Grand Dukes of Tuscany was carried on from Cosimo I. to Gian Gastone, seventh Grand Duke and last of his line, who died in 1737.

The Grand Duchy then passed to the house of Lorraine, and with a Napoleonic usurpation of eighteen years (1796–1814), it continued in the Lorraine family, as represented by the collateral Hapsburgs, till the year 1859. In that year, King Vittorio Emmanuele of Piedmont and Sardinia, entered Florence, which, with all Italy, was united under the Royal Crown of the House of Savoy.

THE TRAGEDIES OF
THE MEDICI

CHAPTER I

The Pazzi Conspiracy

LORENZO—"*Il Magnifico.*"
GIULIANO—"*Il Pensieroso.*"

" *Signori !* " " *Signori !* "

SUCH was the stirring cry which resounded through the lofty Council Chamber of the famous Palazzo Vecchio that dull December day in the year 1469.

Never had such a title been accorded to any one in Florence, where every man was as good as, if not better than, his neighbour. Foreign sovereigns, and their lieutenants, who, from time to time, visited the city and claimed toll and fealty from the citizens, had never been addressed as " *Signori* "—" Lords and Masters." The " *Spirito del Campanile*," as it was called, was nowhere more rampant than in the " City of the Lion and Lily," where everybody at all times seemed only too ready to disparage his fellow.

The cry was as astounding as it was unanimous— " *Signori !* " " *Signori !* " " *Evviva i dué Signori de' Medici !* " " *Signori !* " " *Signori !* " " *Evviva i due figli della Domina Lucrezia.*" Thus it gathered strength —its importance was emphatic—it was epoch-marking.

" *Signori !* " " *Signori !* " was the acknowledgment of the sovereignty of the Medici, made quite freely and spontaneously by the dignified Lords of the Signory, in the name of the whole population of Florence and Tuscany.

The Tragedies of the Medici

Piero de' Medici died on 3rd December 1469, and his interment, which was conducted with marked simplicity, in accordance with his will, was completed that same evening. He had, during his short exercise of power as *Capo della Repubblica*, given a pageant—" The Triumph of Death," he called it, by way of being his own funeral obsequies—a grim anticipation of the future indeed !

At midnight a secret meeting of citizens was convened, by the officials of the *Signoria*, within the Monastery of Sant' Antonio by the old Porta Faenza, to debate the question of filling the vacant Headship of the State. Why such a remote locality was chosen is not stated, but it was in conformity with Florentine usage, which, for general and personal security, required secrecy in such gatherings.

More than six hundred—" the flower of the city " as Macchiavelli called them—attended, and upon the proposition of Ridolfo de' Pandolfini, Messer Tommaso Soderini, by reason of seniority of years and priority of importance, was called upon to preside. " Being one of the first citizens and much superior to the others, his prudence and authority were recognised not only in Florence, but by all the rulers of Italy."

The Soderini had, for three hundred years, held a leading position in the affairs of Florence ; but they were rivals and enemies of the Medici. Indeed Messer Tommaso's uncle—Ser Francesco—was one of the principal opponents in the city counsels of Cosimo—" *il Padre della Patria*." Messer Niccolo, his brother, carried on the feud, and was, with Dietisalvi Neroni, Agnolo Acciaiuolo, and others, banished in 1455, for their complicity in the abortive attempt to assassinate Piero de' Medici.

Messer Tommaso, more prescient and prudent, threw in his lot with the Medici, and was chosen by Piero, not

THE JOURNEY OF THE MAGI (Benozzo Gozzoli.)
CHAPEL OF THE MEDICI PALACE, FLORENCE.

only as his own chief counsellor and intimate friend, but as the principal adviser of his two young sons—Lorenzo and Giuliano. He had, moreover, allied himself to the Medici by his marriage with Dianora de' Tornabuoni, sister of Domina Lucrezia, Piero's wife.

All the same, he kept his own counsel and took up a perfectly independent line of action, being quite remarkable for his display of that most pronounced characteristic of all good Florentines—the placing of Florence first—" *Firenze la prima !* "

At the meeting, at Sant' Antonio, his rising to speak was the signal for general applause. In a few generous words he eulogised the gentle virtues of Piero and bemoaned his premature death. In a longer and more serious oration, on the conditions politically and socially of Florence and of the whole State, he put before his hearers two uncontrovertible considerations, to guide them in the exercise of the selection of a new *Capo della Repubblica*,—first, the maintenance of unity and tranquillity ; and, second, the preservation of the *status quo*.

Many and friendly were the interruptions of the oration, and over and over again shouts were raised for " *Tommaso Soderini il Capo !* " Gracefully he bowed his acknowledgment, but, with much feeling, declined the rare honour offered him. Then he went on to say that as the supreme office had been worthily served by Cosimo and Piero de' Medici, it was but fitting that it should be continued in that illustrious family.

He expatiated upon the advantages which had accrued to Florence under the Headship of the Medici ; and he urged upon the assembly to offer their allegiance to Piero's sons, and to give them the authority that their father and grandfather had possessed.

Keen debate followed Messer Tommaso's speech : some wished that he would reconsider his decision, others were in favour of trying a new man and of another family—Niccolo Soderini's name was freely mentioned, but gradually the meeting came to accept the proposal. It gained at all events the adhesion of such pronounced ante-Mediceans as Gianozzo de' Pitti and Domenico de' Martelli, and led to a fusion, there and then, of the two parties, " *del Poggio* " and " *del Piana*." Unanimity was the more readily reached when those who demurred perceived that Messer Tommaso would be the virtual ruler of the State in the personal direction of his two young nephews. A deputation was accordingly chosen to convey to Domina Lucrezia and her sons the condolences of the city, and to offer to Lorenzo the coveted Headship of the State.

At noon on the following day the deputation was honourably received at the Medici Palace. " The principal men of the State and of the City," wrote Lorenzo in his *Ricordi*, " came to our house to condole with us in our bereavement, and to offer me the direction of the Government in succession to my grandfather and father. I hesitated to accept the high honour on account of my youth and because of the danger and responsibility I should incur ; and I only consented in order to safeguard our friends and our property."

A plenary Parliament was summoned by Tommaso Soderini and those associated with him in the conduct of public affairs during the interregnum. It was held in the great Council Chamber of the Palazzo Vecchio, and was attended by a full concourse of senators and other prominent citizens, deputations from the Guilds, and representatives of the Minor Orders. In the Piazza della Signoria and the adjoining streets, was assembled an immense crowd of people, the greater part being supporters of the Medici.

Inside the Chamber again Messer Tommaso Soderini

The Tragedies of the Medici

was unanimously elected president, and forthwith proceeded to report the result of the deputation. His speech was repeatedly interrupted by cries that he should reconsider his decision and accept then and there the Headship of the State. He again emphatically declined the honour his fellow-citizens desired to confer upon him, and proclaimed Lorenzo de' Medici *Capo della Repubblica Fiorentina.*

At a preconcerted signal the arras over the doorway leading to the private audience chamber was lifted, and there advanced Piero's widow with her two sons, clothed in the dark habiliments of mourning. Domina Lucrezia threw back her thick black veil, revealing upon her kindly face a sorrowful expression and her eyes suffused with tears. Making a lowly courtesy she drew herself up—a queenly figure—and holding the hands of Lorenzo and Giuliano, on either side, made her way to where Messer Tommaso Soderini was standing.

All eyes were bent upon the pathetic little group, and a sympathetic murmur moved the whole audience. Every man of them had for years regarded the Domina as the model of what a woman and a wife, a mother and a queen, should be. She had no rivals and no detractors. Hers had been the wise power behind the throne, for her tactful counsels had guided the actions of her husband unerringly.

Florence was greatly beholden to Domina Lucrezia— a debt which nothing could repay. Her influence for good upon the Court, her munificence in charity, and her unsparing unselfishness had not been without powerful effect upon every one of those hard-headed, hard-hearted citizens. They called to mind that well-known saying of the " Father of his Country "—" the great merchant"—Cosimo : "Why, Lucrezia is the best man among us ! "

5

The Tragedies of the Medici

They reflected, too, upon the auspicious example set at the Palazzo Medici, where the mother's part was conspicuous in the wise training of her family and in the loving deference she received from her sons. And as they gazed upon Lorenzo and Giuliano de' Medici— " the hope of Florence "—they recognised in the former a statesman, already a ruler in the making. Young though he was, he had widely gained a reputation for shrewdness and energy, for Piero had taken his eldest son early into his confidence, and had entrusted to him much important State business. He had sent him with embassies to Rome, Venice, and Naples ; he had despatched him upon a round of ceremonious visits to foreign courts ; and had encouraged him to make himself acquainted with all Tuscany and the Tuscans.

Lorenzo's accomplishments in the school of letters were known to all. He was a scholar and a gentleman, and these points had great weight in Florentine opinion. In figure and physiognomy he very greatly resembled his grandfather. His dignified bearing greatly impressed the assembly, whilst his unaffected modesty, pleasant courtesy, and graceful oratory, gratified them all.

In Guiliano they had a typical young courtier, handsome, athletic, accomplished, and enthusiastic. His physical charms appealed to every one, for most Florentines were Greeks of the Greeks. A precocious boy of sixteen years of age, he had the promise of a brilliant young manhood and a splendid maturity.

The personal equation is always a prominent factor in human ambitions, and nowhere was it more emphatically dominant than in the mutual jealousies of the men of Florence. The "$x + y$" sign of absolute assurance had its match and equal in the "$x - y$" sign of restrictive deference. If one *Messer* arrived at some degree of prominence, then the best way for him to attain his end was to pit himself against another of his class nearest to him in influence. If *he* was not to gain the guerdon, then his rival should not have it !

This was the spirit which permeated the *raison d'être* of each noble lord in that great assembly. After the first wave of enthusiasm had passed, each man began to reflect that the best way, after all, for settling the contentious question of the Headship of the Republic, was to rule every one of the " magnificent six hundred " out of the running ; and by taking the line of least resistance plump for the unassuming youths before them —Medici although they were.

" *Signori !* " " *Signori !* " again ran through the lofty chamber, " *I Signori di Firenze !* " Some cried out " Lorenzo," and some " Giuliano," and others " *I tutte due* "—but shouts for Lorenzo waxed the loudest. Thus by general acclamation was the new *Capo della Repubblica* elected.

Abashed by the vociferations of their elders and yet encouraged by the unanimity of the assembly, the two young men stood gravely bowing their acknowledgments, the heightened colour of their faces and the nervous tension of their frames indicating the fervency of their emotions. In a few well-chosen sentences Lorenzo expressed his pleasure and Giuliano's, and the gratitude of their mother at this signal mark of confidence ; and promised to uphold the traditions of the City and the State, as his forbears had done, craving from the noble lords their united sympathy and support.

Gently leading the now smiling Domina Lucrezia by the hand, the two brothers returned to the private Hall of Audience, while the great bell of the Palazzo boomed forth the news to the waiting crowd outside. The woolworkers had ceased their toil, the artists had left their *botteghe*, the markets were deserted, and all Florence forgathered in the Piazza to welcome " *I Signori di Firenze !* "

Loud plaudits greeted the noble matron and her sons —not the battle-cry " *Palle ! Palle !* " indeed—but " *Evviva i Medici !* " " *Lorenzo !* " " *Giuliano !* " " *La buona Domina Magnifica !* " . . . Their progress was a triumph, they could scarcely make their way, short as it was, to the Via Larga, for everybody pressed forward to kiss and stroke their hands. Never had there been anything like so popular an election in Florence ; men and women shed tears as they uttered rapturously their names ; for were not " Lorenzo " and " Giuliano " the " pets of the people," and was not the Domina Lucrezia beloved by everyone !

The plenary Parliament, having completed its labours, broke up immediately, and the excellent lords and worthy citizens hied them to their palaces, their banks, and their offices, more or less pleased with the morning's work. Not a few reflected, rather grimly, that they had placed two young lives between themselves and the seat of supreme authority. Their sons might live to rule Florence, but their own chances had vanished for ever !

.   .   .   .

Lorenzo was not backward in gripping, with a firm hand, the reins of power. Young as he was, he had already formed his ideals and laid out his plans as to the best government of the State. The yearly symposia in the Casentino had been productive of much good in the training of the youthful ruler. The direction of his opinions was signified in that saying of his : " He who would live in Florence must know how to govern ! "

The repetition of this phrase was perhaps indiscreet, and it caused searchings of heart, as the meaning of it was borne in upon the comprehensions of the least friendly of the citizens. Lorenzo was clearly set upon

UFFIZI GALLERY. FLORENCE.

1. LORENZO.
2. LUCREZIA.
3. CONTESSINA.
4. COSIMO
5. PIERO.
6. GIOVANNI.
7. GIULIANO

The Tragedies of the Medici

the aggrandisement of his house and the dependence of all others. Allowance was made for a lad's impetuosity, but at the same time many a leader kept his hands tightly pressed upon the machinery of government.

Everyone perceived that the young *Capo della Repubblica* was in full possession of the solid grit of his pushful grandfather. He had not studied the careers of his famous ancestors, Salvestro, Giovanni, and Cosimo, for nothing. Indeed Piero, his father, in writing to his sons at Cafaggiuolo to acquaint them with the death of Cosimo, " *Il Padre della Patria*," in 1463, had pointedly said : " Your mother and I offer the character and example of your grandfather to our sons."

Besides these strong characteristics he had inherited, in a superlative degree, the shrewd common-sense of Piero, and his mother's passionate love of Florence, with all her enthusiasm for what was pure, cultured, philanthropic, and religious. Niccolo Macchiavelli, somewhat unwillingly, admitted that—" Lorenzo has all the high-mindedness and liberality which anybody could expect in one occupying such an exalted station."

Giuliano tacitly and contentedly accepted a less ambitious and responsible role. Whilst Lorenzo took the first place and occupied himself in questions of State policy and in the affairs of the family, Giuliano drew to himself all the younger men in physical exploit and mental effort. From boyhood addicted to sports and pastimes, he became *facile princeps* in all manly exercises.

" *Il bel Giulio !* " as he was called generally, was moreover the leader of fashion and the organiser of all the pageants and jousts with which Lorenzo and he delighted the citizens. Whilst devoting most of his time to fun and frolic, the young prince was acknowledged as one of the chief *litterati*, and a conspicuous ornament of the Platonic Academy.

9

The Tragedies of the Medici

The serious side to his character and his studious disposition gained for him the gentle title of " *Il Pensieroso*." His mother's fond hope was that he should be named a Cardinal, not merely a Papal princeling, nor of course a religious reprobate—as, alas, most of the Cardinals were—but a devout wearer of the scarlet hat, and that one day he might even assume the triple tiara!

Anyhow Giuliano's youth was as spotless as it might be amid unchaste surroundings. His passion for the bewitching Simonetta, " The Star of Genoa," seems to have been the only serious romance of his life, and therein he never aroused Marco de' Vespucci's jealousy by his attentions to his young wife. Indeed the loves of " *Il bel Giulio* " and " *La bella Simonetta* " were the talk and the admiration of the whole city :—the Apollo or the Mercury of the New Athens with his Venus— Venus de' Medici !

The magnificent *Giostra*, or Tournament, which Lorenzo celebrated a year before his accession to the Headship of the Republic was but the prelude to the exhibition of lavish hospitality such as Florentines, and the strangers within their gates, had never witnessed. Banquets, ballets and pageants succeeded one another in rapid succession. Church and national festivals gained splendour and circumstance unrivalled in any other city. Indeed the citizens, from the highest to the meanest, lived in a whirl of festivities—and they liked it well!

The visits of friendly princes and other distinguished personages were hailed with enthusiasm. Apparently there was no bottom to the Medici purse ; but actually the *Capo della Repubblica* was playing rather fast and loose with his opulent patrimony. There came a day when the strain grew excessive, and Lorenzo was unable, had he been willing, to make advances to princely suitors, and he lived to repent his prodigality.

The Tragedies of the Medici

The first notable visitors were Duke Galeazzo Maria Sforza of Milan and his Duchess Bona, Princess of Savoy. The retinue which accompanied the sovereigns was gorgeous, and filled the people of Florence with amazement; but their wonder was tenfold greater when Lorenzo displayed still greater magnificence in their reception. Macchiavelli has attributed the vast increase in the luxurious habits of the citizens to this splendid hospitality.

Another remarkable demonstration was that which was made in 1471 upon the occasion of the succession of Cardinal Francesco delle Rovere to the Papal throne as Sixtus IV. Lorenzo, in person, headed the special embassy which was despatched from Florence to congratulate the new pontiff. The other principal members were Domenico de' Martelli, Agnolo della Stufa, Bongianio de' Gianfigliazzi, and Donato de' Acciaiuolo. Whilst the mission and its wealth of offerings were received graciously by the Roman Court, Sixtus by no means extended a cordial welcome to Lorenzo. The request which he made for the bestowal of a Cardinal's hat upon his brother, Giuliano, was refused somewhat brusquely, although, to be sure, the Pope did agree to the transfer of the custody of the finances of the Curia to the Medici bank, through the intervention of Messer Giovanni de' Tornabuoni—Lorenzo's uncle, a resident in Rome.

Lorenzo appears to have made, however, rather a favourable impression upon Sixtus, for he entered into negotiations concerning the sale of the costly jewels which had been collected by Pope Paul II. In the end Lorenzo purchased the cabinet and its contents, and made thereby a very excellent bargain.

During his sojourn in the Eternal City, Lorenzo acquired a number of precious antiques, rare manuscripts, and valuable works of art. Sixtus, noting his artistic tastes, sent him many handsome gifts, and promised, at his solicitation, to prevent the destruction of ancient buildings and monuments. They parted apparently excellent friends.

Giuliano's *Giostra* was even more brilliant than that of Lorenzo, six years before. It was celebrated in honour of " La bella Simonetta," with whom the impressionable young prince became daily more and more madly in love. Whether his infatuation went at all beyond the bounds of Platonic affection is doubtful. His lovely *innamorata* was the wife of his best friend, and his honour went for much in the loyal estimation of Giuliano. Besides this, his good mother's influence in the cause of virtue and modesty was all-powerful with both her sons.

Strange to say, this romantic attachment stirred the jealousy of a very prominent citizen, no less a personage than Messer Francesco de' Pazzi. He and his brothers declined the invitation to the *Giostra*, and abstained from participation in the general festivities. It was a case of race rivalry and of personal jealousy, but it meant much in the relations of the two families.

The efforts which Lorenzo continually made " to gain a firm footing in Florence "—as Francesco de' Guicci-ardini has recorded—quite naturally were productive of opposition and animosity. The men who had placed him in power were again in two camps—those who were content with the *status quo*, and those who were not. The latter made less and less effort to conceal their real sentiments, and at length set about to question Lorenzo's motives, and defeat his projects. He was a *beau-ideal* citizen, for, with all his love of show and circumstance, even in the fulness of his dignity and dominion, he knew how to retain and exhibit certain homely and simple

The Tragedies of the Medici

traits, which were quite after the Florentine manner.

He met criticisms and oppositions with the very characteristic statement : " I will," said he, " allow no man to put his foot on my throat ! " This threat—for so it was accounted by those who wished to discredit him—was like a red gauntlet thrown down, and, later on, a hand—if not a foot—and a dagger, were at Lorenzo's throat!

The overstrain of desire, the feverishness of acquisitiveness, and the lust for power, often in their intensity defeat the purpose sought. The personality of Lorenzo waxed greater and mightier day by day in the nervously articulated constitution of Florence. The greatest genius of his age, he was not only the master of the Government, but the acknowledged chief of the Platonic Academy, the first of living poets, a most distinguished classical scholar, and the greatest benefactor the city had ever known. Everything was within his grasp and everyone had to bow to his will ; his aim was to be autocratic Prince of Tuscany.

It was the mark of a " perfect gentleman " to unbend to plainer folk, and to mingle with them in moments of relaxation. As a youth he had, with Giuliano, frequented the village fairs in the Mugello, for amusement and good fellowship ; indeed they brought him inspiration and popularity as well. When in residence in the Medici Palace he was wont to take his walks abroad quite freely, and to sit and chat with the habitués of the *osterie* by the Porta San Gallo, and other similar taverns.

Florentine of the Florentines, he loved tricks and jokes, and was never tired of making fun at the expense of others : be it said, too, he knew how to take as well as give. An amusing story is told of him : being at Pisa, he chanced to see among the students of the University—which, by the way, he was instrumental in re-establishing and re-endowing—a youth who squinted. He remarked with a laugh : " That lad should easily be the head of his class ! " When questioned as to his meaning, he replied jocosely : " Because he will read at the same time both pages of his book, and so will learn double ! "

Entering thus unostentatiously into the lives and habits of his fellow-citizens, it was perfectly natural that he should gain their esteem, friendship, and loyal support. He soon became out and away the most popular man in Florence, notwithstanding the unworthy sneer of that ill-conditioned and self-opinionated monk, Girolamo Savonarola. " Lorenzo," he muttered, " occupies the people with feasts and shows in order that they may think more of their own amusement than of his ambitions."

Lorenzo was under no delusion with respect to the permanence, in a more or less subjective degree, of the spirit of revolt which had rendered his father's succession to the Headship of the Republic difficult. The very men who had, for their own ends, misguided Piero, of course were no longer powerful—such at least of them as were still alive were in banishment; but their sons and their adjoints were ready enough to question his authority.

Swiftly enough, Lorenzo took the measures of these men, and prepared to counteract their opposition. Naturally he sought the counsel of Domina Lucrezia, than whom nobody understood better the men of Florence, their manners and their moods. Long and serious were the deliberations of mother and son. With her pregnant assistance he roughed out a scheme, so warily conceived and so faithfully elaborated, that, on its presentation to the Lords of the Signory, it was accepted almost unanimously.

This measure touched citizens in their tenderest spot

DUL CE DE CVS

LVCRETIA FRANCISCI TORNABVONI FIL.
VXOR PETRI EX COSMO MEDIC. P. P.

DOMINA MAGNIFICA LUCREZIA DE' MEDICI.

From an engraving by Francesco Allegrini, 1761.

—pride and love of display—for it proclaimed the appointment of the leading *Signori* as ambassadors to foreign courts and communes. The one great absorbing ambition of all prominent Florentines was, through all their history, to head a foreign mission, with all its honours and emoluments.

With infinite grace and persuasiveness Lorenzo put before the Council the advisability of the despatch of envoys, incidentally to announce his succession to the Headship of the State, but principally to proclaim the grandeur, the wealth, and the power, of the great Tuscan Republic. It was a master-stroke thus to appeal to the patriotism, no less than to the egotism, of their Excellencies, and, at the same time, to confirm his own supremacy !

The bait, dangled before avaricious eyes, was eagerly snapped up, and when Lorenzo backed up his proposition by munificently mounting each embassy, and by the promise of knighthood upon the return of the ambassadors, scarcely a man of those nominated held back. The scheme worked splendidly, and Lorenzo had the supreme satisfaction of bidding courteous and thankful farewells to his most prominent rivals.

Among them were such distinguished leaders of public opinion as Bernardo de' Buongirolami, Cesare de' Petrucci, Bernardo del Nero, Agnolo de' Niccolini, and Piero Filippo de' Pandolfini. Their departure was the signal for the advancement of many less known men,— friends and protégés of the two brothers or of Domina Lucrezia. In this way Lorenzo greatly strengthened his hold upon the supreme power.

Two very prominent men, however, rejected the proposal—at once the most popular and most dangerous —Tommaso de' Soderini and Francesco de' Pazzi.

Tommaso de' Soderini added immensely to his

popularity by his noble exhibition of self-abnegation. His prudence and ability had for long pointed him out as the most trustworthy and experienced of his peers. His whole-hearted loyalty to the cause of the Medici, and the consistency with which he maintained the position he had taken up, at the plenary Parliament in 1469, and subsequently, made him, by the contrariety of circumstances, the most redoubtable rival of the ambitious and impulsive *Capo della Repubblica*.

The trusty pilot, who had so effectively steered the ship of State through the troubled waters of the interregnum, was, quite unintentionally and unwillingly, the greatest obstacle in the way of the young captain ! Everybody who had a grievance—real or imaginary —against the government of Lorenzo, sought Messer Tommaso's advice and sympathy, so that the situation became charged with difficulties and embarrassments. The very merest change in the whim of a fickle people might upset the Medici, and then the Soderini would be called upon to fill the vacancy. Messer Tommaso's presence in Florence was both a source of strength to Lorenzo and his house, and a menace.

When the subject of the embassy to Rome—the chief diplomatic appointment of the Republic—was broached, Messer Tommaso, with the utmost sincerity, expressed his fervent wish to meet Lorenzo's views in every respect, but he expressed, quite emphatically, his disinclination to undertake such an arduous duty. Not only did he plead the infirmities of age, but declared that his wife, Madonna Dianora, would never leave Florence. Her love of her own city and its people equalled that of her sister, the Domina Magnifica Lucrezia—their social, charitable and literary interests were alike and equal.

Here was a condition of affairs which called for the exercise of the greatest tact and ingenuity, and Lorenzo committed the task of overcoming the scruples of his uncle and aunt to his mother. Her efforts were entirely successful, and Lorenzo, with a deep sigh of relief, handed Messer Tommaso his credentials, and personally conducted him and his suite to the Porta Romano, and thence speeded him upon his journey.

. . . .

Francesco de' Pazzi was cast in a very different sort of mould—the very antithesis in character, demeanour, and aspiration to Tommaso de' Soderini—he has very appropriately been called " the Cataline of Florence." Possessed of immense wealth, much of which had come to him from his father, Messer Antonio, he rapidly dissipated it by selfish extravagance : no man surpassed him in the virtue or the vice—which you will—of self-seeking.

In the bitterness of an overweening and mortified ambition he rejected, with the utmost discourtesy, Lorenzo's overtures, at the same time remorselessly exposing his intentions, and vowing that no Pazzo should "go round the corner" for a Medico! Messer Francesco displayed unreservedly the true character of his family : he was in truth the " Mirror of his race " —" *L'implacabile Pazzi.*"

The descent of the Pazzi was one of the most ancient among the noble families of Tuscany. The senior branch claimed Greek descent, and its members were early denizens of the hill-country about Fiesole. Leaders of men, they became adherents of the aristocratic party —the Ghibellines—and were consistent and energetic in their allegiance to the Emperor. The junior branch of the Pazzi were dwellers in the Vale of Arno—men of peaceful predilections in agriculture and commerce, throwing in their lot with the Guelphs—the democratic party of the Pope.

Giano della Bella's " *Ordinamenti di Giustizia,*" in

1293, led to the disqualification of the Pazzi and many other notable families from the exercise of the franchise, and, as a consequence, they were deprived of all share in the Government.

They recognised, even in those early days of the formation of the first of modern states, that the Medici were rivals and opponents not only in domestic and commercial enterprise, but also in political advancement, and no love was lost between the two families. Nevertheless, the Pazzi were beholden to their rivals for the restoration of their civil rights.

On the return of Cosimo de' Medici from exile in 1434, they were reinstated, and thenceforward maintained their position. Messer Andrea, next after Cosimo the most influential citizen of Florence, was elected to the Priorate in 1435, and in 1439 he was called upon to entertain no less a personage than King René of France. In 1441 he was *Gonfaloniere di Giustizia*.

Messer Andrea left three sons—Piero, Giacopo and Antonio. Piero served the supreme office of *Gonfaloniere* in 1462. He was the father of a numerous family— some historians say he had nineteen children by his wife, Madonna Fiammetta de' Guigni! None of them, however, made their mark in the life and history of the city, except the fourth son, Belforte Renato, who was a prominent man but suffered for the ill-doings of his relations.

If Piero and his sons were unassuming citizens, Messer Andrea's second son, Giacopo, was of a very different disposition. A man of far greater ability and more vaulting ambition than his brother, he was looked upon as the head of the family. In appearance he was prematurely old and withered up, with a pallid face and palsied frame, with great restless, staring eyes. He perpetually tossed his head about from side to side, as though afflicted with St. Vitus' dance. Giacopo was unmarried, a libertine, notorious as a gambler and a blasphemer, a spendthrift, and jealous—beyond bounds —of the popularity and pre-eminence of Piero and Lorenzo de' Medici. He was pointed at as the most immoral man in Florence. In the year of Lorenzo's succession to the place of *Capo della Repubblica*, he obtained by bribery the high office of *Gonfaloniere di Giustizia* as a set-off, but, by an inconsistency as unexpected as it was transparent, he accepted, on vacating office, a knighthood at the hands of his rival.

Cavaliere Giacopo's relations with Lorenzo were fairly cordial, outwardly at least, for as late as 1474, when at Avignon, he wrote several letters to him, full of grateful expressions for favours received and of wishes for a continuance of a good understanding. None of Cavaliere Giacopo's illegitimate children arrived at maturity, and, on account of the failure of his elder brother's sons to achieve distinction, the proud banner of the family was clutched by the hands of the four boys of the youngest of Messer Andrea's sons—Guglielmo, Antonio, Giovanni, and Francesco. Their mother was Cosa degli Alessandri, a granddaughter of Alessandro degli Albizzi, who first adopted the new surname.

The brothers were very wealthy, they had amassed large fortunes in commerce, and their houses extended for a considerable distance along that most fashionable of streets—the Borgo degli Albizzi. The Palazzo de' Pazzi doubtless was commenced by their grandfather, whose emblem—a ship—is among the architectural enrichments. The building was finished by their uncle, Giacopo—it is in the Via del Proconsolo.

As bankers, the Pazzi were noted for their enterprise generally, and for their competition with the Medici in particular. They had agencies in all the chief cities of Europe and the East, but their reputation for avarice

The Tragedies of the Medici

and sharp dealing was proverbial. Perhaps no family was quite so unpopular in Florence. Their traditions were aristocratic, whilst the Medici were champions of the people.

This distinction was referred to by Madonna Alessandra Macinghi di Matteo degli Strozzi, in one of her letters to her son Filippo, at Naples. " I must bid you remember," she wrote, " that those who are upon the side of the Medici have always done well, whilst those who belong to the Pazzi, the contrary. So I pray you be on your guard."

The growing importance of the Pazzi gave Piero and Lucrezia de' Medici much uneasiness, and it is quite certain that the marriage of their eldest daughter, Bianca—" Piero's tall daughter " as she was called— to the eldest of the three brothers, was a stroke of domestic policy by way of controlling the race for wealth and power.

Lorenzo, very soon after his accession to the Headship of the State, " took the bull by the horns " and excluded the Pazzi from participation in public office. It was an extreme measure and not in accordance with his usual tact and circumspection, and of course it produced the greatest ill-will and resentment against him and his administration in every member of the proscribed family.

The situation became greatly embittered when, in 1477, Lorenzo interfered in a law-suit which concerned the marriage dower and inheritance of Beatrice, the daughter of Giovanni Buonromeo. By Florentine law the daughter should have inherited the fortune without demur, under the express will of her father, who died intestate ; but, at Lorenzo's command, the estate was passed on to Beatrice's cousin, Carlo Buonromeo, who was the winner of the second prize in Lorenzo's *Giostra* of 1468. This decision was in direct opposition to

Giuliano de' Medici's opinion, and he did all he could to reassure Giovanni de' Pazzi, Guglielmo's brother, and Beatrice's husband, of friendship and confidence.

These were not the only incidents which followed one another at the parting of the ways of the two families, but the affair of Giovanni and Beatrice was resented with peculiar bitterness by all the Pazzi. " Hence arose," as Francesco de' Guicciardini has testified, " the wronging of the Pazzi ! "

In Francesco, the youngest of the brethren, was exhibited the most violent animosity and hatred. Blessed with superabundant self-conceit, which went so far as to cause him to spend hours a day having his unusually light-coloured hair dressed at the barber's and his face salved and puffed at the apothecary's to conceal his muddy complexion, he was reckoned, in the Mercato Nuovo, as little better than an ill-conditioned *braggadoccio* ! His shortness of stature he sought to atone for by his accentuation of the Florentine pout and the Tuscan strut—he was well known, too, for his contemptuous jokes at the expense of others.

Francesco denounced Lorenzo and his Government with unmeasured scorn, and, careless of restraint, threatened that " he would be even with him, even though it cost him his life." Macchiavelli says : " He was the most unscrupulous of his family." " A man of blood," Agnolo Poliziano called him, " who, when he meditated any design, went straight to his goal, regardless of morality, religion, reputation and consequences."

Early in March he quitted Florence suddenly, giving out that his presence was required at Rome in connection with the affairs of the Pazzi bank. To say that his departure was a relief to Lorenzo is but half the truth, for he was greatly perturbed with respect to the influence which such a passionate and reckless rival would have upon his relations with the Holy See. Francesco was the subject of watchfulness upon the part of the Medici agents in Rome, where Giovanni de' Tornabuoni set himself to thwart any hostile movement which might be made.

Among prominent men with whom Francesco de' Pazzi was thrown into contact were Archbishop Francesco de' Salviati and Count Girolamo de' Riari. The Archbishop and Francesco were no strangers to one another ; their families had risen to affluence and power side by side in Florence, actuated by like sentiments and engaged in like activities—hatred of the Medici was mutual.

Sixtus had proposed, in 1474, to bestow upon Francesco de' Salviati the Archbishopric of Florence, but the *Signoria*, instigated by Lorenzo, refused to confirm his appointment and declined to grant him the temporalities of the See. The Pope yielded very ungraciously to the representations of the Florentine Government and named Rinaldo d'Orsini, Lorenzo's brother-in-law, to the vacancy. This intervention was adduced by Sixtus afterwards as insubordination worthy of punishment, and he did not forget to take his revenge.

The following year Francesco de' Salviati was chosen as Archbishop-designate of Pisa, and again the Florentines objected—being joined by the Pisans, who conspired to prevent him taking possession. The Archbishop was, according to Agnolo Poliziano—the devoted historian and poet-laureate of Lorenzo il Magnifico—" An ignorant man, a contemner of all law—human and divine—a man steeped in crime, and a disgrace to his family and the whole State."

Count Girolamo de' Riari, accounted a nephew of Sixtus, was, like his elder brother Piero and Caterina his sister, a natural child of the Pope. The three were treated with parental affection by the pontiff, and had their home in his private apartments, being waited upon by their unrecognised mother in the guise of nurse and guárdian.

Piero de' Riari was created a Cardinal when a spoilt boy, and became, as a man, infamous for his debauchery and villainy. Sixtus had the effrontery to select him as successor to Archbishop Orsini in Florence, but his action was prompted by a motive, which was firmly fixed in his heart. This was nothing less than the supplanting of Lorenzo de' Medici by Piero or Girolamo ! So far, however, as Cardinal de' Riari was concerned, Sixtus' ambitions were wholly disappointed by his sudden death, due to violent excesses of all kinds.

Like his brother, Count Girolamo, the offspring of illicit lust, and brought up in the depraved atmosphere of the Papal court, was a reprobate ; but Sixtus' vaulting ambition stopped not at character and reputation. He was bent upon the permanent aggrandisement of all the branches of the Delle Rovere family. Casting about for territorial dignity, the Pope set his heart upon the Lordship of Imola, where Taddeo Manfredi of Faenza, being in financial difficulties, had surrendered the fief to the Duke of Milan.

The proposal to bestow the Lordship upon Count Girolamo de' Riari by purchase was warmly resented by the Florentines. Sixtus approached the question in a most underhand and suspicious manner. He knew perfectly well that negotiations were on foot for the acquisition of the property and title by Lorenzo, on behalf of the Florentine Government. Nevertheless he sent a secret mission to Galeazzo Sforza, Duke of Milan, offering the handsome sum of fifty thousand gold ducats, with a proviso, that the Duke should bestow the hand of his illegitimate daughter Caterina upon Girolamo.

The Tragedies of the Medici

By way of adding insult to injury, Sixtus impudently sought a loan from the Medici bank, with which to pay the Duke : this greatly offended Lorenzo and all the leading men in Florence. What made the Pope's conduct more despicable, was the knowledge that he regarded this matter as the first step in a line of policy which aimed at supersession of the Medici by the Riari in the direction of Tuscan affairs—himself being Over-Lord.

The Pope's demand was refused indignantly by Lorenzo, who, in the name of the *Signoria*, administered to his Holiness a severe rebuke for his interference in the affairs of Florence. The relations between the two Governments became strained, but Sixtus was perfectly indifferent to opposition where personal interests were concerned.

His next move was the withdrawal of the Duke of Urbino, his relative, from the military service of the Republic, and his appointment as Commander-in-Chief of the Papal forces. This manœuvre was regarded with alarm by all the Italian States, and a league was formed by Florence, Venice, and Milan, to check Papal encroachments.

Sixtus made overtures to the Duke of Milan to detach him from the alliance, but, apparently, they failed of their object. The Duke was friendly with Lorenzo and had no wish to become embroiled with Florence.

All these plots and counterplots were exactly to the liking of Francesco de' Pazzi, and he laid himself out to make capital out of them. Not only did he encourage the Pope in his inimical policy, but he placed at his command the sum of money which had been refused by the Medici bank. Sixtus was delighted with his new and wealthy adherent, and forthwith gave the presidents of the Medici bank in Rome notice that they no longer retained his confidence as Papal bankers, and that, accordingly, he had transferred the accounts of the Curia to the care of the rival Pazzi house. Upon Francesco de' Pazzi he conferred the accolade of knighthood. This hostile action of course further estranged Lorenzo and the Government of Florence, and, quite naturally, a system of quarrelsome incidents was set up, with a very complete equipment of spies.

Sixtus never concealed his desire for the overthrow of Lorenzo and the subversion of the Florentine Government, and his hostility found a whole-hearted response in the persons of Count Girolamo de' Riari, Archbishop Francesco de' Salviati, and Cavaliere Francesco de' Pazzi. The Pope exulted openly in what capital he could make out of tales and gossip about Lorenzo and his entourage. Two prominent Florentines fomented this factious spirit, Giovanni Neroni—the Archbishop of Florence in succession to Archbishop d'Orsini, brother of the notorious Diotisalvi, who was banished in 1466—and Agnolo Acciaiuolo—also banished the same year, who resided in Rome and was an especial favourite at the Vatican.

Charges of opposition to the policy of the Pope were freely thrown in the teeth of Lorenzo, and some of them were true, for the actions of the Pope led all observant men to the conclusion that he proposed to assume the role of arbiter in the affairs of all the Italian States. On the other hand, Lorenzo's policy was peaceful, his aim being the consolidation of Medicean domination in the affairs of the Republic.

Causes such as these brought about the initiation of the dastardly plot known in history as "The Pazzi Conspiracy." The name is somewhat open to criticism, for, although the Pazzi were the chief instruments employed, and exceeded all others in detestation of the

The Tragedies of the Medici

Medici, the "fore-front and head of the offending" was no less a personage than Pope Sixtus IV.

"His Holiness hates Lorenzo," said Count Girolamo de' Riari ; this was the cue to all that followed. Doubtless the Pope was much in the power of sycophants and adventurers—all immoral rulers are. Each knew his man and held him in the palm of his left hand ; and none were backward in impressing this knowledge upon him.

"We can always make our lord the Pope do as we please," was Archbishop Salviati's very apposite declaration ! It was re-echoed by Francesco de' Pazzi, who added significantly, "and we mean to rid Florence of the Medici."

.   .   .   .

All through the year 1477 the three arch-conspirators were elaborating their plan of action. Possibly Sixtus —and we may give the miscreant the favour of the doubt —at first merely wished to upset the Government of Florence and banish Lorenzo and Giuliano by direct means. When, however, it was borne in upon him that the immense popularity of the Medici would, in the event of their supersession, only lead to their triumphant recall, he agreed that there was nothing for it but the removal of the two brothers in a more summary manner.

This association of Giuliano with Lorenzo was a miserable exhibition of personal spite. He had refused him the Cardinalate simply because he foresaw the succession of a Medici to the Papal throne, whilst he purposed handing over the triple tiara to his son, Cardinal Piero de' Riari. Nevertheless, there was some idea in the mind of Sixtus, which he conveyed to his fellow-conspirators, of making an agreement with Giuliano, that if he would condone the exile of his brother, then his should be the reversion of the Popedom after Cardinal de' Riari !

LORENZO DE' MEDICI — Il Magnifico.
Angelo Bronzino.

UFFIZI GALLERY, FLORENCE.

The Tragedies of the Medici

Some authorities say Giuliano lent a not unwilling ear to those overtures, but a saner view is that expressed by Agnolo Poliziano in an epigram :—

> " Lorenzo—Giuliano—one spirit, love, and aim
> Animate you both—this, truly, I, your friend, proclaim."

Giuliano's love for Lorenzo was, like that of David and Jonathan, " a love surpassing that of women." He consistently submitted his own ambitions to the exaltation of his brother's magnificence.

The cogitations of the leaders of the conspiracy were disturbed by the fact that, however excellent their schemes might be, there was absolute necessity for the co-operation of other influences. Rome unaided could not cope with Florence, backed as she was by France, Venice, Milan, Ferrara, and Mantua. Sixtus consequently broached the subject of the suppression of the Medici to the King of Naples and to the Duke of Urbino —the support of Siena was always assured in any attack on her great rival.

The king had a personal quarrel with Lorenzo, because he had married Clarice d'Orsini in preference to his daughter, whose hand he had, in a way, offered to the young prince. He at once acceded to the Pope's invitation, and, as good as his word, he despatched his son, the Duke of Calabria, at the head of an armed force, professedly to demand prompt payment by the Republic of arrears due to him for service rendered to Florence.

At the solicitation of Sixtus these troops were retained in Tuscany on the pretext that the Papal fief of Imola required protection. Of course the real purpose was a menace to Lorenzo : the force being at hand to strike a swift blow when necessary.

Duke Federigo of Urbino was made more or less conversant with the Papal policy, and with the special

D

question of Lorenzo's removal. He at once rejected the
proposition that resort should be had to violent or secret
measures, and in disgust at Sixtus's conduct, he threw
up his appointment as Commander of the Papal forces.

Whilst Sixtus was making all these military prepara-
tions for the furtherance of his intentions, his co-con-
spirators removed the scene of their activities to the
neighbourhood of Florence, where the Pazzi and Salviati
were at one in their readiness to lay down their lives for
the undoing of the Medici. They first of all took into
their confidence one of the Papal Condottieri, a man of
undoubted courage and ability—Giovanni Battista da
Montesicco, a native of the Roman Campagna—who
was under heavy obligation to Count Girolamo de'
Riari. Of course he was perfectly willing, as became his
calling, to sell his sword for good payment : he further
undertook to enlist his lieutenant, Hieronimo Comiti,
in the cause.

The Condottiere was sent off to Florence to com-
municate to Cavaliere Giacopo de' Pazzi the " idea "
of the three chief plotters, to test his feelings, and, if
possible, secure his adherence. At first the old man was
" as cold as ice "—so Montesicco said in his confession
later on—and declined to take any part in the conspiracy.
After hearing all that was put before him, he enquired
whether Sixtus approved the scheme.

" Why, his Holiness," replied the Condottiere, " has
sent me straight to your Honour to ask your support.
. . . I speak for the Pope."

" Then," said Giacopo, " I am with you."

A few days later Archbishop Salviati and Francesco
de' Pazzi joined Montesicco at Giacopo's country villa,
at Montughi, just beyond the Porta Rosso, on the high
road to Bologna. Consultations between the heads of
the two families, Pazzi and Salviati—were held there,

The Tragedies of the Medici

with the concurrence of a certain number of influential citizens inimical to the Medici.

These meetings were given out as hunting-parties and, to blind their eyes, overtures were made to both Lorenzo and Giuliano to honour the sport with their presence. Needless to say, Francesco de' Pazzi's return to Florence, in company with the unfriendly Archbishop, aroused Lorenzo's suspicions, but he does not appear to have taken any action.

Montesicco was instructed to make himself and his lieutenant familiar with the stage upon which he was destined to play his part of the plot, and especially to observe the persons and the habits of the two Medici princes. Furthermore, he was directed to seek a personal interview with Lorenzo, on the pretence of submitting suggestions, propounded by Count Girolamo, with respect to the acquisition of some *poderi* near Faenza.

Lorenzo received his visitor with his usual courtesy and hospitality, and, whilst he wondered why Riario should depute such a redoubtable warrior to deal with peaceful matters, he never dreamt that foul play was intended. Montesicco was greatly impressed by the Magnifico's ingenuousness and nobility of character, and still more by the evident esteem and affection in which he was held by all classes of the population. He earnestly reconsidered the bargain he had made : " I resolved," he said in his confession, " that my sword should not slay that just man."

The counsels at Montughi were divergent and acrimonious. At length a resolution was agreed to, as offering a suitable and secure locality for the perpetration of the deed in contemplation, namely, to invite Lorenzo to Rome in the name of Sixtus. Such a step would be regarded as a proof that the Pope no longer opposed Lorenzo's government, but that a *modus vivendi* had been reached, agreeable to all parties. Giuliano was to be included in the invitation as well. Of course the hope was entertained that a favourable opportunity would be afforded, during the Papal hospitalities, for the murder of the two brothers.

The Archbishop took the lead in all these deliberations —he and Giacopo de' Pazzi were boon companions. " They made no profession of any virtue," wrote Ser Varillas, in his *Secret History of the Medici,* " either moral or Christian ; they played perpetually at dice, swore confoundedly, and showed no respect for religion."

Confident in the general support of all the members of his family, in any demonstration against the hated Medici, he took into his personal confidence his brother, Giacopo de' Salviati—" an obscure, sordid man "—and his nephew, Giacopo—" a wastrel and a fanatical anti-Medicean."

Among the trustworthy Florentine confederates the Archbishop enrolled Giacopo, son of the famous scholar, Poggio Gucchio de' Bracciolini, originally a protégé of Lorenzo, but " dismissed his service for insolence and rapacity " ; Giovanni Perugino, of San Gimignano, a physician attached to Cavaliere Giacopo's household ; Giovanni Domenico, a bridle-maker and athlete, but " an idle sort of fellow " ; and Napoleone de' Franzesi, a friend of Guglielmo de' Pazzi, Lorenzo's brother-in-law. Another adherent was Messer Giovanni da Pisa, a notary, but " a factious and bad man."

Before leaving Rome, Francesco de' Pazzi and the Archbishop had agreed with Count Girolamo de' Riari to engage the services of two desperadoes in the pay of the Pope—Bernardo Bandino of the Florentine family of Baroncelli, " a reckless and a brutal man and a bankrupt to boot," and Amerigo de' Corsi, " the renegade son of a worthy father,"—Messer Bernardo de' Corsi of the

The Tragedies of the Medici

ancient Florentine house of that ilk. Two ill-living priests were also added to the roll of the conspirators—Frate Antonio, son of Gherardo de' Maffei of Volterra, and Frate Stefano, son of Niccolo Piovano da Bagnore. The former was exasperated against Lorenzo for the reckless sack of Volterra, and because he had taken possession of a valuable alum-pit belonging to his family. The latter was *Vicario* of Monte Murlo, an upstart Papal précis-writer, whose family was plebeian and employed upon Pazzi property in that locality ; he was " a man steeped in crime and a creature of Cavaliere Giacopo de' Pazzi."

So many having been admitted into the secret of the conspiracy, it became a matter of urgent importance that no delay should arise in the fulfilment of the design ; the fear of espionage and leakage was ever present to the minds of the leaders. But what to do, and where, and how, baffled all their ingenuity. At last a lead came, quite unexpectedly from Sixtus himself.

At Pisa was a youth, studying law and philosophy —Raffaelle Sansoni—the son of Count Girolamo's only sister, just sixteen years of age, and " very tender in the heart of the Pope." Early in 1478 Sixtus had preconized him Cardinal of San Giorgio, and added the honour of Legate for Archbishop Salviati's induction to that See —the richest, by the way, in all Italy.

The boy Cardinal, in April, was directed, by Sixtus, to make a progress to Imola on a visit to his uncle and aunt, and to take Florence on his way, for the purpose of paying his respects to Lorenzo. There was, of course, much more in this apparently innocent proceeding than appeared at first view. Francesco de' Pazzi at once obtained Cavaliere Giacopo's permission to offer the hospitality of his villa to his youthful eminence and his suite.

Montesicco was ordered to furnish an escort of cavalry

in the name of the Pope—" men who were perfectly trustworthy and prepared to carry out whatever commands they received."

After the cavalcade had set forth, Francesco sent a message to Lorenzo de' Medici, suggesting that it might be agreeable to all parties if he could see his way to entertain the Cardinal. Both he and the Archbishop who was in the company of the Cardinal, knew very well that the proposition would be cordially entertained by the hospitable Magnifico.

As they had anticipated, no sooner had the news reached Florence that the distinguished visitors were approaching the city, than a dignified deputation of *Signori* set out to meet them, conveying a courteous invitation to be Lorenzo's guests at Fiesole.

A splendid reception was followed by a noble entertainment, whereat all the more notable dignitaries of the city and the principal members of the Platonic Academy assisted. Among the guests of honour were Archbishop Francesco de' Salviati, with the Ambassadors —Giovanni Morino, representing Ferrante, King of Naples; Filippo Sagramoro, the Duke of Milan; and Ercole di Bendio, the Duke of Ferrara. In special attendance upon Lorenzo, and of ambassadorial rank, were the Cavalieri Agnolo della Stufa, Luigi de' Guicciardini, Bernardo de' Buongirolami, and Buongiano de' Gianfigliazzi, and others.

The conspirators were in a state of the highest expectation that Montesicco and his lieutenant would have no difficulty in finding opportunities to effect their dastardly purpose during the festivities. They were doomed to disappointment, for at the last moment, and when the banquet was in progress, it was remarked that Giuliano was absent—he was indisposed and unable to attend the function !

The Tragedies of the Medici

The Sunday following, 26th April, happened to be the name-day of the Cardinal, and he expressed a wish to hear High Mass in Santa Maria del Fiore. Lorenzo announced his intention of personally conducting his eminence to the Duomo, and requested him to honour the Domina Clarice and himself by attending a State dinner at the Medici Palace, in the Via Larga, at the conclusion of the ceremony.

This was much to the mind of the confederates, for, surely, there would be a favourable opportunity for the execution of the plot. In secret session it was arranged that, at the moment of the Elevation of the Host, Giovanni Battista da' Montesicco should stab Lorenzo, whilst Francesco de' Pazzi and Bernardo Bandino should fall upon Giuliano.

The Condottiere, however, firmly refused to commit the double crime of sacrilege and murder, and, point-blank, declined all further share in the conspiracy. Here was an entirely unlooked-for situation, and an alternative plan was not easy to arrange. Francesco de' Pazzi seemed inclined to step into the breach, but detestation of Lorenzo checked his ardour—he would not soil his hands with the blood of such a contemptible tyrant, a menial should administer the blow! There was no lack of volunteers ready to take Montesicco's place, but excessive caution was requisite that no prominent Florentine conspirator should be chosen, lest suspicion should be aroused.

Finally the two clerical members of the conspiracy, Frati Antonio and Stefano, were entrusted with the grim duty. The appointment was quite the best that could be made, because, at the Cathedral, Lorenzo and his immediate entourage would be placed with the clergy, within the choir, whereas to the Pazzi and the other confederates places would be assigned outside the screen, among the unofficial congregation.

The Tragedies of the Medici

Everything was in order, the great bell of the Duomo was sounding its invitation, and the sacred building was packed with worshippers and spectators. In full state Lorenzo, accompanied by Domina Clarice and their Court, led Cardinal Sansoni to his chair of estate by the high altar.

If, as he himself affirmed, Lorenzo was deprived of the pleasure of smell, he had compensation in the greater acuteness of the other four senses, and it must have struck his keen eyes, as he passed to his place, that there seemed to be an unusually large muster of adherents of the Pazzi and Salviati. Probably he reflected that they were there armed in honour of the Cardinal, who was the guest of Cavaliere Giacopo and under the guidance of Archbishop Francesco, as deputy of his Holiness the Pope.

In the vast congregation everybody of importance in Florence was assembled, with two notable exceptions— the mother and the only brother of Lorenzo il Magnifico. The Domina Lucrezia, who had suddenly retired from the prominent position she held at the Court of her son, remained at Careggi with the venerable Madonna Contessina, Cosimo's widow, upon whom she waited with the utmost devotion.

The other absentee was, once more, Giuliano ! Consternation seized upon the conspirators, for the slaughter would not be complete without the shedding of his blood.

The preliminary anthems were being sung as the procession of the celebrant of the Mass, with his sacred ministers moved from the New Sacristy, and every head was bowed before the symbol of the cross. Hesitation on the part of the confederates meant ruin, and, perhaps, death : this no one knew better than Francesco de' Pazzi. Beckoning to Bernardo Bandino, he led the way to the north door of the Cathedral, and hurried off with him to the Medici Palace, not many yards away.

Asking to see the Lord Giuliano, the porter led them into the courtyard, and presently the groom of the chamber conducted them into the young prince's apartment. Giuliano was nearly dressed, and his valet was giving some final touches to his abundant brown hair and to his robes.

" Hasten, my lord, the Mass is in saying, or you will be too late," exclaimed Francesco, " we have come to conduct you to the Duomo." Giuliano was in a gleeful mood, and joked his visitors upon their unexpected attentions. At length he cried out : " Lead on, Pazzo —Medico will follow ! "

Taking him in his humour, Francesco slipped his arm round Giuliano's waist—apparently as a mark of good-fellowship, but really for the purpose of feeling whether he was wearing armour under his blue velvet tunic. With Bandino on the other side, the three made the rest of their way through the dense crowd in the Via Larga, being greeted respectfully by old and young, though many wondered at " *Il bel Giulio's* " unwonted companions.

Entering the Duomo, the three stood a moment whilst a clear course was made for Giuliano to the centre of the congregation. Lorenzo and the clergy and dignitaries within the choir were already upon their knees, ready to prostrate themselves as the celebrant held aloft the Sacred Host. Near Lorenzo were Giovanni de' Tornabuoni, his uncle,—famous for his wealth, influence at Rome, and his probity,—Antonio and Lorenzo de' Cavalcanti, Lorenzo de' Tornabuoni, Marco de' Vespucci, and Filippo degli Strozzi, Chamberlains of Honour, and other distinguished Florentines, and the foreign ambassadors.

The Tragedies of the Medici

No sooner had Giuliano reached the entrance to the choir and was about to genuflect, than Francesco de' Pazzi, who had followed him closely, whipped out his sword, at the very moment of the Elevation, and ran the devout prince through the back ! At the same time Bandino leaped upon him and stabbed him repeatedly in the breast !

It was all the work of an instant, and Giuliano fell over upon his side, his crimson life's blood ebbing swiftly out of nineteen gaping wounds and dyeing his scarlet robe deep purple. Francesco's frenzy was diabolical, for he leaped upon the still quivering body of his victim, and stabbed him again and again—wounding his own thigh in his fury !

Bandino next attacked Francesco Nori, a chief agent or manager of the Medici bank, a man of renown and honour, who vainly threw himself forward to shield his unhappy young patron, and he cut him down to the ground. With a filthy execration, he raised the dripping weapon in the air, prepared for yet another victim.

Meanwhile the two perjured priests, who, by the mock grace of their Order were placed within the choir, had taken up positions immediately behind Lorenzo, as though to render him assistance in the divine service, suddenly attacked him with daggers, but unskilfully. Lorenzo scrambled to his feet, and, casting his heavy mantle of State over his shoulders, drew his sword in self-defence. Turning to see who his opponents were, he received a scratch in the neck from Stefano's steel. Then, from the raised dais, he descried the tumult at the choir gates, whilst cries of " *Il Giuliano e morto* " reached his ears !

Desperadoes were struggling with the clergy and the acolytes by the great lectern, and calling out his name for vengeance. One, more murderous than the rest, was

GIULIANO DE' MEDICI — Il Pensieroso.
Angelo Bronzino.

UFFIZI GALLERY, FLORENCE.

scaling the low sanctuary wall, holding his gory dagger in the air, and making for the chairs of estate—it was Bernardo Bandino. Commending the Domina Clarice to the care of his uncle, Lorenzo passed hurriedly up the steps of the altar and gained the New Sacristy, followed closely by the two Cavalcanti, who were battling with the infuriated Bandino and his confederates—" *Abbasso il Lorenzo*," they yelled.

Escaping through the doorway, Luca della Robbia's great bronze gates were slammed to, by Angelo Poliziano, almost crushing Antonio Cavalcanti, who fell with a deep wound in his shoulder, and actually flinging to the ground, outside in the aisle, the raging, baffled Bandino.

" Then arose," wrote Filippo Strozzi, in his family *Ricordi*—he was an eye-witness of the tragedy—" a great tumult in the church. Messer Bongiano and other knights, with whom I was conversing, were stupefied, one fled hither and another thither, loud shouts filled the building, and the hands of friends of the Pazzi and Salviati all held gleaming weapons. . . . The young Cardinal remained alone, crouching by the high altar, until he was led away by some priests into the Old Sacristy, whence he was escorted by two of the ' Eight,' with a strong bodyguard, to the Palazzo del Podesta."

Inside the New Sacristy it was discovered that Lorenzo's wound was serious enough to call for immediate treatment, and one of his devoted pages, young Antonio de' Ridolfi, sucked it for fear of poison. The great heavy metal doors were incessantly battered from without, but no one dared to open them, and Lorenzo remained where he was until the hubbub in the Duomo appeared to be abating. Then another page, Sismondo della Stufa, climbed up into the organ gallery, whence he could look into the church, and reported that none but friends of the Medici remained, and they were crying out for Lorenzo to accept their escort to the palace. So the Magnifico departed.

All the while the great bell of the Palazzo Vecchio was booming out its dread summons for the city trained bands and the armed members of the Guilds to assemble for the defence of the city and the maintenance of their liberties. Loud cries of " *Liberta!* " " *Liberta!* " rolled up the street, drowned by a great chorus of " *Evviva le Palle!* " " *Abasso i Traditori!* " The whole city was in an uproar and blood was being spilt on every side.

What had happened was tragically this. Whilst one half of the conspirators was told off to strike the fatal blow, the other half was directed to rally round Archbishop Salviati, who, by the way, made some excuse for not assisting ministerially at the Mass, but took up his station close to the north door of the Duomo. Directly they saw Giuliano struck to the ground, they made all haste to the Palazzo Vecchio, and demanded an interview with Messer Cesare de' Petrucci, the *Gonfaloniere di Giustizia*, who had been detained by urgent matters in the Courts.

When Messer Petruccio enquired the nature of their business, the Archbishop replied: " We are come, all the family of Salviati, to pay our respects to the *Gonfalo-niere*, as in duty bound." Messer Cesare was at lunch, but, rising from the table, he welcomed the Archbishop, who entered the apartment alone. He asked him to be speedy, as he had to join the banquet to the Cardinal di San Giorgio almost immediately.

Salviati said he was the bearer of his family's greet-ings to the *Gonfaloniere*, and also of a private Brief to him from the Pope. His manner seemed so strange and his errand so irregular, that Petruccio's suspicions were aroused, and raising the arras, he saw the passage was filled with armed men. At once he called the palace guard to arrest the intruders, and caused every door of exit to be locked.

The object, of course, of the Archbishop and those with him was to seize the person of the *Gonfaloniere* and possess themselves of the Banner of Justice—that they might rouse the citizens to fight in its defence.

On the contrary, the people were for the Medici, and " *Palle !* " " *Palle !* " prevailed. Noting that the Salviati did not leave the palace, and that the guards had been withdrawn from the gate and every door was bolted, the populace broke into the building, rescued the *Gonfaloniere*, and the *Signori* with him, and seized the persons of the intruders.

Without more ado they ran the miscreants, Francesco, Giacopo, and Giacopo di Giacopo de' Salviati, Giacopo de' Bracciolini, and Giovanni da Perugia, up to the lantern of the Campanile, and, thrusting their bodies through the machicolations, hung them head downwards ! Others of the party and some of the Cardinal's servants, who had accompanied the Archbishop, were flung from the windows.

Cavaliere Giacopo de' Pazzi was neither at the Duomo, nor did he accompany the Archbishop to the Palazzo Vecchio. His part was to await news from Salviati that he had seized the *Gonfaloniere* and the palace, and then to ride fully armed with a retinue of mercenaries and Montesicco's bodyguard of the Cardinal to the Piazza della Signoria. Without awaiting the signal he advanced, raising the cry " *Liberta !* " " *Liberta !* " but none rallied to his side.

Instead, he and his escort were pelted with stones and, on arriving in the Piazza, he beheld the gruesome human decoration of the Campanile. Without a moment's hesitation, spurring his horse, he rode

swiftly towards the Porta della Croce, and set off into
the open country—a fugitive !

Francesco de' Pazzi, after the slaughter of Giuliano,
escaped to his uncle's house, and stripping himself,
received attention to his wound, which was of a very
serious nature. He was not, however, left very long in
peace, for the cry had gone forth in the streets—" Death
to the traitors ! " " Down with the Pazzi and the
Salviati ! " " Fire their houses ! " The sword, still
reeking red with the bluest blood of Florence, was
swiftly crossed by the sword of retribution. Francesco
was dragged forth, naked as he was from his bed,
buffeted, pelted, and spat upon, they thrust him with
staves, weapons, hands and feet, right through the
Piazza della Signoria ; up they forced him to the giddy
gallery of the Campanile, and then, flinging his bleeding,
battered body out among his bloodthirsty comrades,
they left him to dangle and to die with them there !

The Archbishop, still in his gorgeous vestments,
turned in fury, as he hung head downwards in that
ghastly company, and, seizing his fiendish confederate,
fixed his teeth in his bare breast, and so the guilty
pair expiated their hellish rage—unlovely in their lives,
revolting in their deaths !

.   .   .   .

Poor Giuliano's corpse was left weltering in his blood,
where he had been done to death, outside the choir
screen of the Duomo. At length he was picked up
tenderly by the good *Misericordia*. His terrible wounds
were reverently washed and his godlike body prepared
for sepulture. News of his assassination had been
swiftly carried out to Careggi, and Domina Lucrezia,
bracing herself for the afflicting sight, hastened to lay
his fair head in her lap, a very real replica of " *La
Pietà* "—Blessed Mary and her Son.

Ah ! how she and the women who bore her company wept for the beloved dead. Ah ! how with tender fingers they counted each gaping wound. Ah ! how gently they cut off locks of his rich hair, as memorials of a sweet young life.

They buried Giuliano that same evening, with all the honours due to his rank, amid the tears of an immense concourse of people—stayed for a while from their savage man-hunt. To the Medici shrine of San Lorenzo they bore him—the yellow light of the wax candles revealing the tombs of Cosimo and Piero.

" There was not a citizen," says Macchiavelli, " who, armed or unarmed, did not go to the palace of Lorenzo in this time of trouble, to offer him his person and his property—such was the position and the affection that the Medici had acquired by their prudence and their liberality."

Lorenzo came out on the loggia, and addressed the people massed in the street. He thanked them for their devotion and assistance, but entreated them, for his dear, dead brother's sake, to abstain from further atrocities and to disperse to their homes in peace.

Nevertheless, all the Pazzi and Salviati were proclaimed " *Ammoniti*," and they were pursued from house to house, whilst the peasants took up the hue and cry in the *contado*. Bleeding heads and torn limbs were everywhere scattered in the street ; door-posts and curb-stones were dashed with gore ; men and women and the children too, were all relentless avengers of " *Il bel Giulio's* " blood. It is said that one hundred and eighty stark corpses were borne away by the merciful *Misericordia* and buried secretly !

Cavaliere Giacopo, who had escaped into the hilly country of the Falterona, near the source of the Arno, was recognised by a couple of countrymen, who were frequenters of the markets in Florence. They seized him and took him to the city gate, where they sold him for fifty gold florins. His shrift was short, for his purchasers, adherents of the Medici, hacked off his head in the street, and carried it upon a pole to the Ponte Vecchio !

Buried at Santa Croce, in the chapel of the Pazzi, his mutilated body was not left long in its grave. It was pulled up, denuded of the shroud, and, with a rope tied round the feet, dragged by men and women and even children to the Lung' Arno, and pitched, like a load of refuse, into the dusky river !

Several of the arch-conspirators hid for a while in various places, mostly in convents, but their time came for punishment. The two priests, Antonio and Stefano, were, two days after the tragedy in the Duomo, brought out of the cellars of the *Badia* of the Benedictines at Santa Firenze, and killed, not swiftly and mercifully, but tortured and mutilated to the satisfaction of the rabble.

Bernard Bandino, after picking himself up at the New Sacristy doors, immediately realised the failure of the conspiracy, and, wise man that he was, put his own safety before all other considerations. He worked his way through the struggling crowd in the Cathedral and got out by the south portal. Luckily enough, the Cardinal's horse had been left tethered by its affrighted groom hard by, so without awaiting news from the Archbishop, he vaulted into the saddle and made off at a hand gallop to the Porta Santa Croce.

With more cunning than Giacopo had shown, he made, not to the Tuscan hills, but to the Tuscan sea, and reached Corneto just in time to board a ship bound for the East, and at the point of weighing anchor. At Galata he went ashore and communicated with Sixtus, who sent him a goodly sum of money and sundry Papal safeguards, with his blessing !

There he lay hid for many weeks, but, as luck would have it, one day he came out of his lair in a Turkish divan, and encountered an agent of the Medici, who recognised him, followed him, and charged him before the Pasha. Put in irons by the Sultan's command, communication was made with Lorenzo. An envoy was despatched to Constantinople, to whom the wretch was handed, and, two months after his crimes in Santa Maria del Fiore, his living body was added to the string of stinking corpses, upon the side of the Campanile, which still dangled in their iron chains, betwixt earth and heaven, rained on and withered by the elements, and fed upon by carrion !

All the seven sons of Piero de' Pazzi were banished for life. They seem to have had no very intimate knowledge of the conspiracy ; indeed, they were all away from Florence, except the fourth, Renato, and he was beheaded " for not having revealed the plot, he being privy to the treachery of his uncle Giacopo and his cousin Francesco."

Renato, indeed, tried to escape, knowing that he was implicated, although not engaged in the plot, but the garrison of Radicofani discovered him and his hiding-place, and he was despatched under guard to Florence.

Giovanno de' Pazzi, Francesco's brother, who had married Beatrice Buonromeo, hid, for a time, in the monastery of Degli Angeli, and then, with his wife, was banished to the castle of Volterra, where he died in 1481. It does not appear that he took any active part in the plot, although his wronging by Lorenzo was the spark which fired the whole conspiracy.

Guglielmo de' Pazzi, the husband of Bianca de'

The Tragedies of the Medici

Medici, Lorenzo and Giuliano's sister, was protected by *Il Magnifico*, and allowed to reside in a villa twelve miles outside Florence.

Napoleone de' Franzesi, alone of all the conspirators, effected his escape, but Piero de' Vespucci, father-in-law to " *La bella Simonetta* "—" *Il bel Giulio's* " *innamorata*,—who assisted him, was sentenced to two years' imprisonment in the Stinche, with a heavy fine.

Giovanni Battista da Montesicco's fate was, perhaps, the only one which excited commiseration, even from the point of view of the Medici. A soldier of fortune, his weapon was at your command, did you but fill his pouch with ducats of Rome or florins of Florence. To him it mattered not whether the adventure partook of romance and espionage, or of intrigue and murder. Unlike many of his profession, he was a religious man, and just. He drew back from his bargain as soon as he had experience of Lorenzo's character, and he refused point-blank to slay him in a spot " where Christ could see him," as he said.

It does not appear that he was inside the Cathedral that dread April morning, but remained on watch to see what transpired. On the defeat of the conspiracy he fled, with many more, right out of Tuscany. Agents of the Medici, however, pursued him and, having captured him, dragged him back to Florence. Before the Lords of the *Signoria* he made confession of what he knew of the conspiracy and of his own part therein. On 4th May, just seven days after the tragedy, he paid the penalty of his misplaced devotion, and he was hanged within the Palace of the Podesta.

Two arch-conspirators are still to be accounted for, Pope Sixtus IV., and Count Girolamo de' Riari ! The former never expressed the least regret or concern at the tragic occurrences in Florence, but openly deplored the failure of his scheme to replace Lorenzo by Girolamo. Furthermore, he issued a " Bull," which began : " Iniqui- tatis filius et perditionis alumnus," and ended by anathema of Lorenzo, whereby he was excommunicated, and all Florence placed under an Interdict !

Moreover, he laid violent hands upon Donato Accia- iuolo, the Florentine ambassador, and, but for the prompt intervention of the envoys of Venice and Milan, would have cast him, uncharged, into the dungeons of the Castle of Sant Angelo. The majority of the Florentine merchants in Rome were arrested, their property confiscated, and to add insult to injury, Sixtus demand- ed from the *Signoria* the immediate banishment of Lorenzo. He expressed his keen sorrow for the deaths of the Pazzi and Salviati, his " devoted sons and trusty counsellors." He spoke of the execution of the Arch- bishop as " a foul murder caused by the tyranny of the Medici," and he put a price upon the head of Cesare de' Petrucci, the *Gonfaloniere di Giustizia !*

As for Count Girolamo, who had, coward-like, kept in the background—he was probably little more than a complacent tool in the hands of the pontiff—he was permitted to leave Florence in the train of the young Cardinal, immediately before the reception of the Inter- dict. He returned to Rome and abandoned himself to a life of profligacy ; his palace became a brothel and a gambling hell, and there he lived for ten years, dishonoured and diseased. His retributive death was by the hand of an assassin in 1488.

The failure of the plot, whilst it added tremendously to the popularity of the Medici and strengthened still more Lorenzo's position, threw the Pope frantically into the arms of the King of Naples. He persuaded him to join in a combined and powerful invasion of Tuscany. At Ironto the Neapolitan troops crossed the frontier and encamped, whilst the Papal forces moved on from Perugia and Siena.

Lorenzo at once called a Parliament to consider the position, and to take steps for the protection of the city and the defence of the State. He addressed the assembly as follows : " I know not, Most Excellent Lords and Most Worshipful Citizens, whether to mourn or to rejoice with you over what has happened. When I think of the treachery and hatred wherewith I have been attacked, and my brother slain, I cannot but grieve ; but when I reflect with what eagerness and zeal, with what love and unanimity, on the part of the whole city, my brother has been avenged and myself defended, I am moved not merely to rejoice, but even to glory in what has transpired. For, if I have found that I have more enemies in Florence than I had thought I had, I have at the same time discovered that I have warmer and more devoted friends than I knew. . . . It lies with you, my Most Excellent Lords, to support me still, or to throw me over. . . . You are my fathers and protectors, and what you wish me to do, I shall do only too willingly. . . ."

All the hearers were deeply affected by Lorenzo's oration, some indeed shed tears, but all vowed to support him in resisting the enemy at the gate. " Take courage," they cried, " it behoves thee, Lorenzo, to live and die for the Republic ! "

At the same time they enrolled a bodyguard of twelve soldiers, whose duty it should be to accompany Lorenzo whenever he went abroad, and to protect him in his palace or at his villas. Doubtless they thought the Pope might resort to further secret measures for the slaughter of his enemy.

Thus ended the terrible " Conspiracy of the Pazzi."

CHAPTER II

The First Tyrannicide

IPPOLITO—" *Il Cardinale.*"
ALESSANDRO—" *Il Negro.*"
LORENZINO—" *Il Terribile.*"

" Go at once, ye base-born bastards, or I will be the first to thrust you out—Begone ! "

These were the passionate words of the proudest and most ambitious princess that ever bore the great name of Medici—Clarice, daughter of Piero di Lorenzo—" Il Magnifico," and wife of Filippo di Filippo degli Strozzi —" Il Primo Gentiluomo del Secolo."

They were spoken on 16th May 1527, in the Long Gallery of the Palazzo Medici, in Florence, and were addressed to two youths—sixteen and thirteen years old respectively, who shrank with terror at the aspect and the vehemence of their contemner. Clarice was a virago, both in the Florentine sense of man's equal in ability and action, and in the sense of the present day—a woman with a mighty will and endowed with physical strength to enforce it.

The two " bastards " were Ippolito, the natural son of Giuliano de' Medici, Duke of Nemours, and Alessandro, the so-called illegitimate son of Lorenzo de' Medici, Duke of Urbino, the virtual ruler of Florence. The lads were not alone in their exposure to the wrath of Madonna Clarice, for, sitting in his chair of estate, was

47

The Tragedies of the Medici

Silvio Passerini, Cardinal of Cortona, their Governor, and Pope Clement VII.'s Regent of the Republic.

" Begone " ! Well had it been if the Cardinal had taken his charges right away from Florence never to return.

.   .   .   .

" The splendour, not of Tuscany only, but of the whole of Italy has disappeared ! " wrote Benedetto Dei, in his *Cronica*. " The Burial Confraternity of the Magi laid his body in the sacristy of San Lorenzo, and the next day the funeral obsequies were held without pomp—as is the custom of the *Signori*—but quite simply. Truly it may be said that however gorgeous the ceremonies might have been, they would have proved altogether too mean for so great a man."

This relates to the death of Lorenzo il Magnifico, which occurred on 8th April 1492. That year is one of the most memorable in modern history : Columbus discovered America ; Roderigo Borgia was elected Pope ; Charles VIII. became the most prominent political figure in Europe ; and the power of Florence had reached its zenith.

She was not only the Head of the Tuscan League and the chief Republic in Europe, but also the first of modern states. If the spirit of the Greeks inspired the physical prowess of the Romans, the enlightenment of the Florentines brought forth the renascence of the arts and crafts of Italy and of the world.

Cosimo, " *Il Padre della Patria*," laid the foundation-stone of Medici renown in the iron grip of his powerful personality, and Piero, his son, maintained unimpaired its eminence by his urbanity and good sense. To Lorenzo, however, was reserved the distinction of placing upon that mighty column its magnificent copestone, and he adorned it with the sevenfold balls of his escutcheon, whilst on the summit he held unfurled the great Red Cross Oriflamme of Florence.

Lorenzo left three sons and three daughters to uphold that ensign and to exhibit the glory of their house. To the first-born, Piero, came the great inheritance of his father's place and power, and no man ever entered into a greater possession,—a possession, so firm, so unquestioned and so portentous, that nothing seemed likely to disturb its equilibrium or to sully its triumph.

But, " the son of his father is not always his father's son," and this quaint saying is perfectly true of Piero de' Medici—a youth of twenty-one years of age—the exact age of his father on his succession to the Headship of the State. Physically the young prince was well favoured, he was cultured and, like his unfortunate uncle Giuliano, he was an adept in all gentlemanly exercises.

Alas, he took not the slightest interest in politics, nor in the business affairs of his house, and the proverbial urbanity and pushfulness of the Medici were alike absent. Whilst he lightly handed over to Piero Dorizzi di Bibbiena, his Chancellor, the conduct of public affairs, he listened to the proud persuasions of his mother, to whom anything like commercial pursuits were abhorrent. Clarice d'Orsini's forbears had all been soldiers, Lorenzo's merchants, that made all the difference in Rome's degenerate days.

Of course there was no Florentine girl good enough to be the bride of young Piero de' Medici—at least, Domina Clarice, his mother, decided so. She was the proudest of the proud, and as ignorant and prejudiced as she was haughty. Her son could only wed a Roman princess, and, by preference, a daughter of the Orsini ; consequently Alfonsina, daughter of Roberto d'Orsini, Clarice's cousin, entered Florence in state on 22nd

May 1488, for her magnificent nuptials with the young *Capo della Repubblica*.

The same year the Domina died. Her influence had not been for good, and her want of tact and her unpopularity caused Lorenzo much anxiety. Perhaps, however, a prince of his conspicuous and, in many ways, unique ability, was better mated with an unsympathetic spouse than with a woman who could, from parity of gifts, enter into his feelings and aspirations. He lived for the magnanimous renown of Florence —she for the selfish prominence of her family.

Francesco de' Guicciardini wrote of Piero de' Medici thus : " He was born of a foreign mother, whereby Florentine blood got mixed, and he acquired foreign manners and bearing, too haughty for our habits of life." The prince gave up most of his time to pleasure and amusement with the young nobles of his court, and encouraged the aims and ambitions of the self-seeking scions of his mother's family. At a single bound the immense personal popularity of Lorenzo, his father, disappeared. Florentines took the young ruler's measure, and he was found wanting.

The imprisonment and threatened execution of his cousins, Lorenzo and Giuliano de' Medici, was a flagrant mistake. The three had quarrelled about Lorenzo il Magnifico's pretty daughter, Luigia, but it was a baseless rumour that she had been poisoned. Bad blood was made always in Florence by such romances and such interference.

In September 1494, Charles VIII. crossed the Alps, and, whilst Savonarola fanatically hailed his coming to Florence as " God's Captain of Chastisement," politicians of all parties looked to Piero to show a bold front and resist the French invader as commander-in-chief of a united Italian army.

IPPOLITO DE' MEDICI — Cardinal.
Vecellio Tiziano.

PITTI PALACE, FLORENCE.

The Tragedies of the Medici

Piero made no sign, but went on playing *pallone* in the Piazza Santa Croce. The enemy seized the Florentine fortresses of Sargana, Sarzanello and Pietra Santa. The news sobered the headstrong, self-indulgent prince for the moment, and then craven fear seized his undisciplined mind. In a panic he mounted his horse and, attended only by two officers of the city guard, he galloped off to King Charles' camp.

In the royal tent Piero fell upon his knees, craved forgiveness for Florence's opposition, and pleaded for generous terms for himself and his fellow-countrymen. Charles demanded the cession absolutely of the three fortresses, with the cities of Pisa and Livorno, and with them the "loan" of 200,000 gold florins ! Piero's report was listened to in solemn silence by the *Signoria*, but when its tenor was conveyed to the concourse of citizens, outside the Palazzo Vecchio, cries of " *Liberta!*" " *Liberta !* " rent the air.

When Piero rode out of the Piazza, accompanied by an armed escort, he was met by an exasperated mob who assailed him with missiles and stones. The big bell, up in the Campanile, began to speak its ominous summons, and, in reply to faint cries of " *Palle !* " " *Palle !* " renewed shouts of " *Liberta !* " " *Liberta !* " proclaimed the abdication of the Medici.

A Parliament was convened and five ambassadors were appointed to treat with Charles and revoke Piero's surrender. One of them, speaking for the rest, denounced him as "No longer fit to rule the State"—it was Piero de' Capponi. The *Signoria* passed a sentence of expulsion upon Piero and his brothers, and placed a reward of two thousand gold florins upon his head, and five thousand more, if he and Giovanni, his Cardinal brother, were captured together.

Needless to say, before the decree was promulgated

The Tragedies of the Medici

Piero and Giovanni flew precipitately through the Porta San Gallo, upon their way to Bologna, at the head of a few mercenaries, and with them went Piero's chancellor.

An enraged mob of citizens rushed pell-mell into the Via Larga, sacked the Palazzo Medici, and scattered the treasures which Piero and Lorenzo had gathered together. The streets were strewn with costly furniture, carpets and tapestry, and priceless works of art were either burnt or broken in pieces. It was not a question of looting but of destruction, and for eighteen years the building was a mark for obscenities and imprecations.

The French army marched through the humiliated city, and terror filled the hearts of the people. Charles occupied a portion of the palace, which the *Signoria* hastily put into some sort of order, borrowing or buying furniture and other articles for his use.

On their knees, an entirely new experience for the proud Florentines, the *Signoria* besought the Emperor's clemency. He took a high hand with them, demanding a huge indemnity and threatening to command his trumpets to sound for pillage. One man alone asserted his liberty, a man who throughout Piero's short government had voiced the public discontent—Piero de' Capponi—the most capable soldier Florence possessed. Boldly and alone he faced the Conqueror and denounced his demands. He tore in pieces the fatal document of Piero's capitulation, flung the pieces in Charles' face, and defied him, saying, " If you sound your trumpets we shall ring our bells ! "

Charles was cowed, he signed a treaty of peace with honourable terms for Florence, and left the city, after a stormy scene with Savonarola. " Take heed," the latter said, " not to bring ruin on this city and upon thyself the curse of God ! "

The Tragedies of the Medici

Piero outlived his cowardly surrender and shameful flight three years—an outcast from his country and a disgrace to his family. He found an asylum in the house of his wife Alfonsina's father, Roberto d'Orsini, Count of Tagliacozzo and Alba. In 1502 he entered the service of the King of France, the enemy of his country, against the Spanish conquerors of the kingdom of Naples. The French were worsted and took to their ships at Gaeta. Piero escaped, but his death followed shortly, for the boat in which he was crossing the River Garigliano, or Liri, near the famous stronghold of that name, was swamped by the fire of the Spanish artillery and he was drowned. Cambi, who relates the history, sententiously winds up his narrative with the apposite words, " Thanks be to God ! "

After Savonarola's death in 1498, Piero de' Soderini was placed at the head of the Government as *Gonfaloniere di Giustizia*, whilst Piero's brother, Cardinal Giovanni, took up the leadership of his discredited party. The terrible sack of Prato in 1512 was an opportunity for the Medici, which they did not neglect to use to their advantage. In terror the Florentine Government paid 140,000 gold florins to the Spanish Viceroy and commander, who made it a condition of his evacuation of Tuscany, that the Medici should be recalled as private citizens, and be granted permission to purchase back their forfeited property. On 12th September of the same year, Giuliano, the third son of Lorenzo il Magnifico, with his young nephew, Lorenzo, Piero's son, entered Florence, attended by a small following. He was one of the noblest of his race, but he was wholly lacking in initiative and energy. He made no claim to political eminence, and his self-abnegation led to the return to Florence of his more pushful brother, the Cardinal, who was accompanied by

53

The Tragedies of the Medici

Giulio de' Medici, the bastard son of the murdered Giuliano. They installed themselves in the restored palace, assumed much of the wonted state of their family in bygone days, and were accorded public recognition and honour.

The following year Cardinal Giovanni was elected Pope as Leo X., and, at the same time, Giuliano was created Duke of Nemours—a dignity bestowed by Francis I. of France—and Lorenzo became Duke of Urbino. The conferring of these titles stirred the rancour of a considerable number of ambitious *Signori*, and intrigue and plots to upset the rising fortunes of the Medici were rife. The very next day after the death of Pope Julius II., Bernardo de' Capponi and Pietro Papolo de' Boscoli were condemned to be hung within the Palace of the Podesta, for an attempt upon the lives of Giuliano, Lorenzo, and Giulio de' Medici. Eighteen accomplices were tortured and many others banished : Niccolo Macchiavelli was implicated in the conspiracy, but he appears to have escaped punishment.

Quietly but persistently the power of the great family was recovered. " The Pope and his Medici " became a proverb throughout Italy : all men noted their rising fortunes and their bids for power. Giulio was preconised Cardinal, Giuliano appointed *Gonfaloniere* of the Papal army, and Lorenzo became the virtual Head of the Florentine Republic. Giuliano died in 1516, Lorenzo in 1519, and Pope Leo X. in 1521. The first left no legitimate offspring, and the second only one daughter, Caterina, besides a natural son, Alessandro.

.   .   .   .   .   .

Upon the death of Lorenzo, Duke of Urbino, Cardinal Giulio de' Medici hastened to Florence, where he was permitted to assume almost autocratic control of State

affairs. Possibly he was regarded in the light of Regent
for Lorenzo's only legitimate child, Caterina. He had
undoubtedly personal fitness for the post of Chief of
the Republic. During the brief period, barely five
months, of his administration, he did very much to
place public interests upon a firm and practical basis.

Very adroitly he played off the "*Ottimati*," under
Pietro de' Ridolfi, against the "*Frateschi*," led by
Giacopo de' Salviati, without identifying himself with
either party. Recalled to Rome on the death of Leo
X., he left Cardinal Silvio Passerini of Cortona his
deputy : a man useful as a tool but of no ability or
judgment. Adrian VI., who succeeded to the Papacy,
was a weak pontiff, and Rome became a hot-bed of
intrigue and villainy.

A plot to assassinate Cardinal de' Medici failed, and,
in 1523, he was, after many weeks of wrangling, elected
Pope, with the title of Clement VII. In the Vatican,
that "refuge for bastards and foundlings," room was
found for two boys, cousins, each the offspring of a
Medici father, but illegitimate. They were brought up
under the immediate eye of the Pope, indeed one of
them, the younger, was said to be the son of Clement.

Ippolito, just fourteen years old, was the bastard
son of Giuliano de' Medici, Duke of Nemours. His
mother was a noble lady of Urbino, Pacifica Brandini,
but she permitted her child to be exposed in the streets,
in a basket, where he was rescued, and taken into the
foundling ward of the Confraternity of Santa Maria di
Piano d'Urbino. There the kindly Religious gave
him the name of "Pasqualino," indicative of the
Church season of Easter, when he entered surrep-
titiously upon the world's stage.

When the child was less than two years old the nuns
of Santa Maria were removed to Rome, and they took

The Tragedies of the Medici

with them, along with other unfortunates, little Pasqualino. Upon a visit, which Pope Leo paid to the convent, he noticed the young boy, and as he smiled and tried to get at his Holiness, Leo was struck with his good looks and made enquiries about his origin. In the end, Leo undertook the little fellow's education and maintained his interest in him, and, moreover, ordered his name to be changed to Ippolito.

Alessandro—the younger boy—twelve years old, was the son of Lorenzo de' Medici, created Duke of Urbino in 1536, when the Pope annexed that principality to the pontifical estates, upon the excommunication of the rightful sovereign. His mother was a woman of colour, a Tartar slave girl, who passed for the wife of a *vetterale* or courier, in the pay of the Duke. He was a native of Colle Vecchio, near Riete, in Umbria, and went by the name of Bizio da Collo, whilst the girl was simply called Anna. Alessandro, later on, was made to feel the baseness of his origin, for he was greeted contemptuously as " Alessandro da Colle Vecchio ! " His supposed father, Bizio, died in 1519, but Cardinal Giulio de' Medici adopted him.

The two boys grew up together at the Vatican, alike in one respect only, their mutual hatred of each other. They were, indeed, as unlike as two boys could be. Ippolito, as the child of gentle parents, had an aristocratic bearing. He was a clever lad and excelled especially in classical learning, in music and poetry. In appearance he became remarkably handsome, with polished manners and a fondness for spending money and for ostentation.

Alessandro, on the other hand, exhibited the attributes of his low-born mother. Physically well-made, he was dark of skin, with dark, curly hair, thick lips, and close-set Eastern eyes. His tastes were unrefined.

He had none of Ippolito's gentleness and attractiveness but in disposition he was morose, passionate, and cruel. His manners were marked by abruptness and vulgarity. He was no genius, and refused to receive the lessons of his masters, and set at defiance all who claimed authority. Alessandro was a shrewd lad all the same, and became Clement's inseparable companion—no doubt he was his son !

Everybody noticed the mutual affection between " uncle " and " nephew," which gave clear indication of a nearer relationship. Clement's word was Alessandro's law, and, when the cousins fell out, as they did many times a day, the interference of their uncle brought peace, but for Ippolito dissatisfaction, as he was usually ruled to be in the wrong. This boyish rivalry led to more considerable emulation and the proprieties of the Papal palace were rudely shaken by the quarrels and the struggles of the cousins.

They were parted and removed each to a remote portion of the palace, with separate suites of attendants, and their only meetings took place in the private apartments of the Pope, and rarely. Thus Ippolito and Alessandro entered upon their teens with no judicious, kindly, or formative influences round them. It was said that each boy threw in the other's face the fact of his illegitimacy, which fawning dependants had revealed to them. Their environment and associates were most undesirable, and nothing was done to instil and encourage sentiments of honour, self-control, truthfulness, and charity. Their initiation into the hypocrisies of spiritual life and ecclesiastical duty produced distaste and contempt for religious exercises.

There was yet another protégée of Clement's left upon the world of mutability and chance—an orphan child, the only issue of Lorenzo, Duke of Urbino and his wife Maddalena, daughter of Jean de la Tour d'Auvergne et de Bourbon. Married in 1518, the delicate young mother died in childbirth the following year, leaving her sweet little baby girl, Caterina, to the care of her brokenhearted husband.

The future Queen of France was placed with the foundling nuns of the convent of Santa Lucia in the Via San Gallo. Thence she was removed to the convent of Santa Caterina di Siena, back to the nuns of Santa Lucia once more, and then handed over to the charge of the noble convent of S. Annunziata delle Murate until 1525, when her aunt, Madonna Clarice de' Medici, wife of Messer Filippo negli Strozzi, was constituted her guardian and instructress.

Right well the new *governante* carried out the instructions of Clement, and she only relinquished her charge when the Pope commanded the young girl, just eleven years old, to Rome. Apartments were provided for her and her suite in the Palazzo Medici, where Madonna Lucrezia, Lorenzo il Magnifico's daughter, and wife of Giacomo de' Salviati, was appointed her protectress.

Without a mother's care, and tossed about here and there, Caterina grew up devoid of high principles, and became the toy of every passing pleasure and indulgence. All the eligible princes of Europe were, in turn, supposed to be her admirers, and rivals for her hand and fortune. And truly the last legitimate descendant, as she was, of the great Cosimo, was a prize in the matrimonial market—if not for her beauty and her virtues, at all events for her wealth and rank. Indeed, there was a project, seriously entertained, seeing that the elder line of the Medici had failed to produce a male heir, of acknowledging Caterina as "*Domina di Firenze*," with a strong council of Regency to carry on the government in her name.

The Tragedies of the Medici

This proposal did not gain any favour outside the Papal cabinet : in Florence it was scouted with derision. Two violent politicians, if not more, lost their heads over the young girl's destiny—Battista Cei, for proposing that she should be placed in the lion's den, and Bernardo Castiglione, for demanding that she should be put upon the streets of Florence, wearing the yellow badge of woman's shame !

In Rome Caterina conceived at once an invincible repugnance for Alessandro—her father's son. His appearance, his manner, his language appalled her ; probably she was not long before she knew the story of his birth. On no account would she speak to him, and, if he entered an apartment where she happened to be, she rushed out, crying, " *Negrello—Bastardo !* "

With Ippolito, on the contrary, she was the best of friends. She admired the good-looking boy, his talents for music, and his skill in gentlemanly exercises. The Venetian ambassador at the Vatican remarked, in a letter to his Government : " We have here a little Medici princess, Caterina, the only child of the late Lorenzo, Duke of Urbino. She and Don Ippolito, the bastard son of Duke Giuliano, are inseparable companions. The boy is very fond of his young cousin, whilst she is devoted to him. She has confidence in nobody else, and she asks him only for everything she wants." Ultimately, of course, Caterina de' Medici became Queen of France, as the consort of Henry II.

The trend of affairs in Florence gave Pope Clement grave anxiety, for, of course, his own personal control became less and less effective upon his elevation to the Papacy. Accredited representatives of the family were required to be in residence there for the maintenance of Medici supremacy. Alas, legitimate male heirs of the senior branch from Cosimo, " *Il Padre*

F

della Patria," were non-existent, and Giovanni delle Bande Nere and his family would not, had he been chosen as *Capo della Repubblica*, consent to be dependent upon Rome.

Clement took counsel with the Florentine ambassadors, who had been sent to congratulate him upon his elevation. Very adroitly he placed by his chair of state the two youths, who passed for Medici, and who were " as dear to him as sons "—Ippolito and Alessandro. In compliment to the Pope, and certainly not from conviction, the fourteen envoys agreed in asking him to send the two boys to Florence, under the charge of a worthy administrator, who should hold the reins of government in Clement's name.

Delighted with the success of his stratagem, Clement chose the Cardinal of Cortona, one of his most obedient and faithful creatures, to accompany Ippolito, nearly sixteen years old, to Florence as quasi-Regent for the lad. With them went, as Ippolito's chamberlains, four Florentine youths of good birth who were favourites of the Pope, Alessandro de' Pucci, Pietro de' Ridolfi, Luigi della Stufa, and Palla de' Rucellai.

The cortège was received in Florence without demonstrations of any kind ; but certainly Ippolito made a very favourable impression by his good looks and gaiety. The Cardinal and his companions drew rein first at the Church of the SS. Annunziata, where they heard Mass, and they then rode on to the renovated Palazzo Medici. A meeting of the *Signoria* was convened, and by a narrow majority Ippolito was declared eligible for the offices of State.

The appointment of Passerini was unfortunate. " He was," writes Benedetto Varchi, " like most prelates, extremely avaricious ; he had neither the intellect to understand the Florentine character nor the judgment to manage it, had he understood it." Ippolito assumed at once the style of "Il Magnifico," and began to display a lust for power and a taste for extravagance quite unusual in so young a lad. The Cardinal yielded to every whim, and very soon a goodly number of courtiers rallied round the handsome youth.

Having launched one of his protégés successfully upon the troubled sea of Florentine politics, Clement despatched Alessandro, under the care of Rosso de' Ridolfi, one of his most trustworthy attendants, with little Caterina de' Medici. They were instructed to report themselves to Cardinal Passerini, and then without delay to proceed to the Villa Poggio a Caiano.

This was a very wise arrangement on the part of Clement, in view of the strenuous rivalry and emphatic dislike the two lads had for each other. The two were kept apart as they had been at the Vatican, but this led naturally to the creation of rival parties and rival courts, each of which acclaimed their respective young leaders as *Il Capo della Repubblica* and " *Il Signore di Firenze.*" Better far as matters turned out, had it been deemed sufficient to advance Ippolito alone. His splendid talents—although linked to fickleness and inconsistency—and his liberality, appealed to the Florentines, and he might have proved a second Lorenzo il Magnifico.

The sack of Rome in 1527 and the imprisonment of Clement VII. in the fortress of Sant Angelo, raised the spirits of the Republicans of Florence. Niccolo de' Soderini, Francesco de' Guicciardini and Pietro de' Salviati took up a strong position as leaders of a popular party, and once more the cry of " *Liberta !*" " *Liberta !*" was raised. Cardinal Passerini was advised to leave Florence and to take the two lads with him.

Among those who escaped from Rome were Filippo

The Tragedies of the Medici

negli Strozzi and his wife Clarice. They posted off to
Florence, and whilst Filippo temporised with the
Cardinal and with the party of reform on either hand,
Clarice declared openly for the opponents of her own
family.

She attended a specially convened meeting of the
anti-Medicean party, and placed her services at their
disposal. It was arranged that she should visit the
Cardinal the following day. Dressed superbly, wearing
the family jewels, and conveyed in a State sedan-chair,
she proceeded to the Palazzo Medici—the house of her
fathers. Ippolito and Alessandro, with their tutors
and attendants, met her upon the grand staircase,
and conducted her to the presence of the Cardinal.

Standing in the Long Gallery, she poured forth a
torrent of scornful words upon the baseborn scions of
her family. " My Lord," she cried, " my Lord, to
what a pass has my family sunk. Do you think that
any of my great ancestors would have borne you so
long. Alas ! that my race has none but female legitimate offspring." Then turning to the astonished lads
she continued : " You had better both look out for
yourselves and go away before the Cardinal here
destroys you and Florence ! "

Some of the suite tried to interfere and to pacify
the enraged woman, but to no avail, she went on
vehemently to denounce the intrusion of the two
bastards.

" Begone, you who are not of the blood of the Medici,
both of you, from a house and from a city to which
neither of you, nor your patron, Clement—wrongfully
Pope and now justly a prisoner in Sant Angelo—have
any legitimate claim, by reason of birth or of merit.
Go at once, ye baseborn bastards, or I will be the first
to thrust you out ! "

Her hearers quailed under her invective, and Passerini humbly promised to quit the palace, but when Clarice had gone he sent for Filippo negli Strozzi and expostulated with him. Filippo's apology was as quaint as it was effective. " Had she not been," said he, " a woman and a Medici, he would have administered to her such a public chastisement as would have gone bad with her ! " He nevertheless, strongly advised the Cardinal to depart, and he conveyed the intelligence that the lives of the two lads were by no means secure, and that should anything happen to them, the Pope would demand them at his hands.

On 29th May 1527, Cardinal Passerini, with Ippolito and Alessandro and their suite, accompanied by Filippo, rode out to Poggio a Caiano, amid the execrations of the populace. Thence they departed for Rome, where the young men lived more or less quietly for two years in Clement's private apartments at the Vatican.

.　　.　　.　　.

In spite of Ippolito's superiority of appearance, manners and attainments, the Pope made no concealment of his preference for Alessandro. He created him Duke of Citta di Penna—a fief within the Papal States—and decided that the riches and greatness of the House of Medici should be continued in Alessandro and not in Ippolito.

" Ippolito," wrote Varillas, " was seized with incredible grief and indignation, and it seemed to him, that being older, a nearer relation to the Pope, and better endowed by nature, so rich an inheritance should rather be his . . . either not knowing or not believing the rumours that Alessandro was Clement's son."

Goaded by what he conceived to be a legitimate ambition, Ippolito posted off to Florence with the idea of seizing the executive power. Clement despatched Baccio Valori after him, with entreaties and promises, and finding that he had no welcome among the Florentines, Ippolito returned quietly to Rome.

The Pope immediately, and without consulting him, preconised him Cardinal—greatly to his disgust. He had no wish for ecclesiastical preferment, he was a soldier at heart, and meant to be ruler of Florence. Clement noted the young man's partialities—he was only just twenty years of age, and he encouraged him in his extravagant tastes by liberally endowing his Cardinalate. A Brief *" In commendam "* was bestowed upon him, whereby the revenue of all vacant benefices and Papal dignities, for six months, were transferred to his account. Moreover, in 1529, he was appointed Archbishop of Avignon, Legate of Perugia, and Administrator of the See of Casale. These fat endowments very considerably affected Ippolito's position. In Rome he had a Court of three hundred notable personages of all nations; his most intimate friends were soldiers and statesmen of renown, and writers and artists of the highest abilities and fame.

Clement having placated Ippolito, set to work to carry out his plans for Alessandro. He wrote on his behalf to the Emperor Charles V. to invite him on his way from Flanders, whither he had travelled to avoid disputes with Ippolito, to visit the Imperial Court. Charles received Alessandro with great honour, and expressed his pleasure at greeting the near relative of the Pope.

A treaty was subsequently signed at Barcelona between Charles and Clement, whereby it was agreed that Alessandro should espouse Margaret, Charles' illegitimate daughter, and that Clement should create Florence a Dukedom in favour of Alessandro. At the

The Tragedies of the Medici

same time the Emperor was asked to intercede between the rival cousins but he naively replied, "Neither wants liberty but aggrandisement ! Let them be."

Alessandro entered Florence on 5th July 1531 accompanied by Giovanni Antonio Muscettola, envoy and chancellor of the Emperor. He proceeded to the Palazzo Vecchio, there he read aloud the injunction of Clement, countersigned by Charles, which established him as Duke of Florence. The office of *Gonfaloniere di Giustizia* was abolished, and the *Signoria* restricted in their powers as merely consultative authorities. At the same time the Republic was superseded and the citizens allowed to exercise the franchise only in the election of civil magistrates.

The *coup d'état* was complete and meekly enough the *Signoria* declared that—" Considering the excellent qualities, life and habits of the most illustrious Duke Alessandro de' Medici, son of the late Magnificent Lorenzo, Duke of Urbino ; and in recognition of the many and great benefits received, both spiritual and temporal, from the House of Medici, he was eligible for all the offices of State."

Alessandro at once began to follow the bent of his base inclinations. As supreme Head of the State he ruled autocratically, and set justice and decency at defiance. The Florentines abashed by the pass in which they found themselves, seemed powerless to oppose the Duke's aggression upon their liberties. That had come to pass against which they had striven for hundreds of years—Florence was subject to *Il governo d'un solo*.

Significantly enough, Alessandro took as his motto " *Un solo Signore, una sola Legge,*" and this he stuck up all over Tuscany. He applied it quite autocratically by disarming the citizens, building fortresses, banishing

The Tragedies of the Medici

the disaffected nobles, and confiscating all properties he coveted. These were but the beginnings of troubles.

Taxes were doubled, every office at court was held by a creature and toady of the Duke, bribery and corruption of all kinds ruled the State, and there appeared to be no limit to his lust and rapacity, and no barrier against the chicanery of his adherents.

Added to all this was the dislocation of public order. Florence became a hot-bed of immorality and a sink of iniquity. Women were openly ravished in the streets, the inmates of convents were not spared, men were wronged and removed suspiciously, the eyes and ears of the children were assailed by unblushing depravity. The *oubliettes* of the Bigallo had their fill of victims.

" Tyrant of Florence " was the designation which best fitted the new ruler. He destroyed the fabric of society and polluted the sanctity of family life. Dismay and revenge alternated in the feelings of the people. Those who dared, began to flock to Ippolito, who, with grim satisfaction, received at his palace in Rome all disaffected refugees. Meetings were held at Filippo negli Strozzi's house, and a movement was set on foot for the overthrow of Alessandro and his dissolute government. A deputation was sent to the Emperor Charles to complain of the tyranny of the Duke and to expose his immoral life. This sealed Ippolito's fate, for Alessandro at once took steps, not only to checkmate the action of the deputation, but to circumvent the destruction of his rival.

Clement had of course full knowledge of the condition of affairs in Florence, and of the increase of hostility between the cousins, but both he and Paul III., who succeeded him as Pope in 1534, kept Ippolito engaged in military and diplomatic duties away from Italy.

Knowing his predilection for soldiering, he was despatched, at the head of eight thousand horsemen, to
the assistance of the Emperor against the Turks who
had invaded Hungary under the Sultan Soliman.
His valour and ability were remarkable ; and the dash
with which he marched, later on, to the defence of
Rome, marked him as a commander of rare distinction.

Returning once more to Rome, he abandoned himself
to a career of debauchery and extravagance. Catillo,
his castle-villa at Tivoli, became the resort of immoral
and disreputable persons. The Pope sought to redress
the disorder : he owed much to Ippolito at the time
of his election to the Papacy, which was in a great
measure achieved by his keen advocacy, so he sent
him on embassies to the Emperor at Barcelona, and
to the King of Naples, under promise of rich revenues.

At the castle of Fondi, near the little town of Itri
in the Neapolitan province of Terra di Lavoro, eight
miles from the fortress of Gaeta, and overlooking the
high road from Rome to Naples, was living, in strict
retirement, a girl greatly beloved by the Cardinal.
Guilia Gonzaga, such was her name, was the attractive
and clever daughter of Messer Vespasiano Colonna,
whose brother, Cavaliere Stefano, had taken a prominent and honourable part in the defence of Florence
during the memorable siege of 1529-1530.

Guilia was certainly only one of the many eligible
maidens proposed at various times as a wife for the
young ecclesiastic : but, in her case, the betrothal was
all but affected, and with the approval of Pope Clement,
whose conscience smote him when he saw that his
handsome and gay young nephew was anything but
disposed to observe the conventions of his Order.

Nevertheless, the lovers were parted, and Guilia
was confined in the conventual fortress, and carefully

guarded. Pope Paul, it appears, did not relax the imprisonment of the unfortunate girl, as he surely ought to have done, in recognition of the Cardinal's successful advocacy of his own advancement.

Naturally, poor Guilia pined and pined for her lover with whom she was of course forbidden to correspond. At length her health gave way, and she appealed to her father to obtain just one interview with Ippolito before she died. Reluctantly permission was given by the Pope, and Ippolito, after the completion of his diplomatic duties in Naples, sought the neighbourhood of his *innamorata* ; ostensibly upon the plea that his health needed the rest and change which the invigorating air of the *Foresteria*, a sanatorium at Itri, offered.

Among Guilia's attendants was an old retainer of Alessandro de' Medici, still devoted to his service, and mindful of youthful escapades together at the Vatican. Him Alessandro persuaded, by means of a heavy bribe and the promise of efficient protection, to undertake the removal of Ippolito. Whilst dallying with his former mistress, the Cardinal fell ill of malarial fever, common in the swampy plain of Garigliano, where he had gone shooting snipe.

Giovanni Andrea da Borgo San Sepolcro, the accomplice of his master, prepared some chicken broth, which he persuaded Ippolito to take. In spite of its bitter taste he partook largely, but during the night he was attacked with immoderate sickness. Before morning dawn the brilliant career of Ippolito, Cardinal de' Medici, ended, and the harvest sun of 10th August 1535 rose upon his rigid corpse in Guilia's chamber !

The poisoner fled to Florence, and was lodged safely in the Palazzo Medici, under the Duke's special protection. Alessandro received the news of Ippolito's death with the utmost satisfaction. " Now," said he,

ALESSANDRO DE' MEDICI.
First Duke of Florence. (Giorgio Vasari.)
UFFIZI GALLERY, FLORENCE.

" the vile wasp is crushed at last ! " The dead body of his victim was buried hurriedly at Itri, but, by Pope Paul's direction, it was exhumed and given honourable burial within the church of San Lorenzo-e-Damaso in Rome. Paul lamented the tragedy which had removed his friend so cruelly, and he boldly accused Alessandro of having brought it about.

No one died more regretted. All Rome was in deepest mourning, and great and small thronged to his burial. He had played the part of Lord Bountiful ungrudgingly and with indiscriminating liberality. Very fittingly it was remarked that he bore as his motto " *Inter omnes.*" He had all the making of a great man, but fickleness, inconsistency, impatience, and self-indulgence, belittled his reputation. Nevertheless, his character shone resplendently when contrasted with that of his rival Alessandro.

Ippolito de' Medici left a son by his mistress, Asdrubale, who became a soldier and a knight of Malta.

Neither Pope nor Emperor made any very energetic protests to Alessandro, but were busy with anxious personal enterprises—and self-interests usually exclude any other. True, Charles wrote to the Duke and questioned him about the death of Ippolito, and required that all the facts of the case should be laid before him, but the matter ended there. Alessandro made no reply !

In six months the sensation had blown over, and the Emperor visited Florence in gorgeous State on 24th April. He was royally entertained by Alessandro, but he made no friends among the nobles, and departed without bestowing the usual honours. The Medici Palace had been redecorated, and it witnessed a revival of the lavish hospitality of Lorenzo il Magnifico.

Margaret of Austria entered the city for her marriage

The Tragedies of the Medici

with Alessandro on 19th July 1536. She came from
Naples accompanied by the Vice-Queen and Cardinals
Santi Quattro and Cibo. The nuptial Mass was sung
at San Lorenzo, and then the whole city was given
over to feasting and debauchery. "The young Duchess
was serenely happy, for the Duke paid her great court,
and she knew not that he paid as much to other women
of all grades!" Banquets, masked balls, street
pageants, *Giostre*, and musical comedies crowded
one upon another.

Among the wedding guests was Lorenzo di Pierfran-
cesco de' Medici, who held the Lordship of Piombino,
the lineal descendant and heir of Cosimo, "*Il Padre
della Patria's*" brother Lorenzo. His father died
when he was an infant, but his mother, Maria de'
Soderini—a woman possessed of all the prudence and
culture of her family—devoted herself to his rearing
and education. Just twenty-three years old, he was
small of stature and slightly built, dark complexioned,
and of a melancholy aspect. His health was indifferent
and he was liable to uncontrollable fits of passion : he
was restless and dissatisfied, and the associate of low
and evil companions.

In Rome—where he had lived in the Medici "happy
family" of the Pope—he acquired the reputation of a
coward and a provoker of disturbances. He was fond
of defacing and mutilating ancient monuments, and
became liable to pains and penalties from which
Cardinal Ippolito rescued him. By his depraved and
foolish habits he greatly incensed Clement, who at
length dismissed him in disgrace. Lorenzo retired to
Florence, where he was welcomed and entertained by
Alessandro.

In return for favours Lorenzo, nicknamed in Florence
"*Lorenzino*," "Lorenzo the Little," became useful

to the Duke and appointed himself spy-in-chief of the Florentine exiles. His studious character and his literary talent endowed him with another and a worthier sobriquet " *Filosofo*," and he carried out the rôle by dressing as a Greek and living as a sybarite. Devoted to the study of the classics and encouraged by his sensuous tutor, Giovanni Francesco Zeffi, when not engaged in vulgar orgies, he translated Plato and other writers, and even composed a comedy, which he called *L'Aridosio*.

Lorenzino entered fully into the Duke's life of profligacy and became his inseparable companion. Both of them admired physical charms and indulged in all physical passions : they set a base fashion in Florence, which degraded her men and women. They habitually made lewd jokes of everything human and divine, and were noted for their cruelty to animals. If Alessandro became execrated as " The Tyrant and Ravisher of Florence," Lorenzino was scouted as " A monster and a miracle," and his depreciative nickname underwent a new spelling—" *Lorenzaccio*,"—" Lorenzo the Terrible! "

. . . . .

Satiety of excesses produced a revulsion of feeling between the two debauchees. Alessandro began to show irritation at his companion's freedom. The latter refused to be corrected, and into his mind came once more the inspiration of classical heroes of liberty and foes of oppression. Why should he not be a Florentine " Brutus," and have his name engraved upon the pinnacle of fame as the " Saviour of his Country ! " Lorenzino studied and studied well the part he now set himself to play.

Not a word did he breathe to man or woman of what was paramount in his mind, and he made not the slightest difference in his intercourse with Alessandro—

indeed, he drew himself to him more intimately than ever. The Carnival of 1536 saw the maddest of all mad scenes, and everything and everybody ran wild riot. Disguised as country minstrels and mounted upon broken-down donkeys, the two comrades rode about the city, paying visits to their various mistresses and flatterers, and playing practical jokes upon the respectable citizens they encountered.

Returning one evening, weary with their follies, they supped together at the Palazzo Medici, and then Lorenzino inquired how they were to spend the night.

" I shall go to bed," replied Alessandro, " for I am worn out."

" Caterina ? " whispered Lorenzino.

Alessandro rose abruptly and said, " Lead on, Lorenzo, I will follow."

Seeing his valet and confidant, Guistiniano da Sesena, he said : " We are going to Signore Lorenzino's, but what shall I put on ? "

Guistiniano handed him a crimson silk dressing-gown, and asked him whether he would wear his sword and steel gauntlets, or whether his cane and his scented kid gloves would not be more suitable.

" Yes," the Duke replied, " toss me over my lovers' gloves, for I am about to see my lady ! "

Snatching a cloak, lined with fur, and grasping a light sword in his hand, Alessandro left the palace by the garden wicket, followed by his valet and two secret guards, Giomo da Carpi, and an Hungarian wrestler nicknamed " Bobo."

Meanwhile Lorenzino had sought the street, and at the corner he found his usual attendant, Michaele del Tovallaccino, a soldier possessed of a splendid physique, combining the soft contour of Apollo and the brute force of Hercules. His comrades called him " Scoronconcolo," on account of his wild, lustful nature. " He could kiss and bite," they said, " at the same time ! "

" Michaele," said Lorenzino, " I want you to kill the man who is my greatest enemy."

" My lord," replied the ruffian, " I am at your service. Tell me the name of the fellow who has wronged you and I will kill him right off. I would kill Jesus Christ himself if he hated you ! "

" Stay at your post and I will return for you presently," said Lorenzino, going on to his own house across the way.

In the Piazza San Marco he overtook Alessandro, who dismissed his attendants, and went on alone with his cousin. In Lorenzino's chamber was a good fire, and Alessandro, complaining of the heat, loosened his attire and removed his sword, handing it to Lorenzino, who deftly entangled the sash and belt in the hilt and placed it upon the bed.

" Where is Caterina ? " inquired the Duke. " Why is she not here ? "

" She is quite ready," was the reply, " and only awaits me to conduct her hither."

" Go at once and delay not ! " cried Alessandro.

Locking the door from without, and putting the key in his pocket, Lorenzino hastened to Michaele.

This " Caterina " was Caterina Ginori, Lorenzino's mother's sister. Forced by her father, Paolo d'Antonio de' Soderini, to renounce her lover, Luigi degli Alamanni, and to marry Leonardo de' Ginori—a disreputable spendthrift and gambler, who fled to Naples to escape his creditors—she attracted the notice of Duke Alessandro. She was as accomplished as she was beautiful and very commanding in appearance, the mother of Bartolommeo, the giant manhood model of Giovanni da Bologna for his famous " Youth, Manhood, and Age," miscalled " The Rape of the Sabines," in the Loggia de' Lanzi.

At the rendezvous Lorenzino slapped Michaele upon the shoulder. " Brother," he said, " the moment has arrived. I have locked my enemy in my room. Come on, now is your opportunity."

" March ! " was the ruffian's terse reply.

" Don't fear to strike," said Lorenzino, as they strode on side by side. " Strike hard, and if the man should seek to defend himself, strike still harder. I trust you."

" Never you fear, my lord, were the man to swear he was the Duke or the Devil, it matters not. Strike I will, and hard."

Mounting the stairs quietly, Lorenzino opened the door of his apartment softly, and there lay Alessandro, fast asleep upon the bed, with his face to the wall. Coward, as he was wont to call himself, he no longer feared to slay the " Tyrant of his People," but whipping out his sword, not waiting for Michaele's attack, he thrust it right through the Duke's back !

With a frantic yell Alessandro stumbled upon the floor. " Traitor ! assassin ! " he screamed. Then, turning his eyes full upon Lorenzino, he faintly added : " This from thee—my lover ! "

Alessandro made as though to defend himself, and with the red blood gushing from his back, he threw himself upon his murderer and they struggled on the floor.

Michaele was powerless to strike : his weapon might have slashed his master. Alessandro, with dying energy, seized the hand of Lorenzino and bit two of his fingers to the bone, so that the miscreant yelled with agony. Then they parted—Lorenzino to bind up his broken bones and Alessandro to staunch his wound.

The Tragedies of the Medici

" At him," cried the madman, and Michaele struck at him with his sword, cutting off his right cheek and his nose, and then he got his dagger at his throat, and turned it round in the gaping wound, until he nearly decapitated his unhappy victim. Again Lorenzino heaved at him with his reeking weapon and fell upon him, covering himself with blood, and bit his face in savage rage ! Alessandro fell away and lay, breathing heavily in a fearsome heap. Then Lorenzino, chuckling with fiendish glee, roared out, " See, Michaele, my brother, the wretch is dead ! "

Raising the body of the still breathing Duke, his murderers threw it upon the bed and covered it with the sheets. Then Lorenzino opened a window and looked out upon the Via Larga, to see if anybody was about. Not a soul was there. It was early morning, and by the new light of day he tore off a piece of paper and scribbled upon it, with Alessandro's blood, " *Vincit amor patriæ laudumque immensa cupido*," and pinned it over Alessandro's heart !

Both he and Michaele washed their hands and their swords—their clothes they could not cleanse—and Lorenzino, having filled his pouch with the money and jewels he possessed, they picked up their cloaks and hats, and, locking the door behind them, departed. In the basement they encountered Fiaccio, Lorenzino's faithful body-servant, groom and valet combined, and he was bidden to follow his master.

The three made their way with haste to the residence of Bishop Angelo Marzi, the chief custodian of the City Gates, of whom Lorenzino demanded post-horses, showing to the servant Alessandro's signet-ring, which he had pulled off his victim's finger. The Bishop made no demur, being well accustomed to the erratic ways of the cousins. They took the road to Bologna, where

75

The Tragedies of the Medici

Lorenzino had the two broken fingers removed, and his hand dressed, and then on they posted without further halt.

Lorenzino made at once for the house of Filippo negli Strozzi, the leader of the exiled Florentines in that city, and rousing him from his slumbers, embraced him with emotion, and said : " See, this is the key of the chamber where lies the body of Alessandro. I have slain him. Look at my clothes, this blood is his, no more shall Florence suffer at his hands. Revenge is sweet, but freedom is sweeter ! "

Filippo could scarcely believe the glad tidings, and surveyed his visitor from head to foot. Lorenzino, noting his hesitation, called Michaele into the room crying, "Here is Scoronconcolo the Assassin, and I am Lorenzaccio the Terrible ! "

" Thou art our Brutus, my Lord Lorenzino ! " exclaimed Filippi, with tears running down his cheeks. " Tarry awhile, till I can summon our chief allies, and rest yourselves. Bravo ! Bravissimo ! "

Next day alarm spread through the Medici Palace when the Duke failed to make his appearance, especially as at noon he had summoned a meeting of his new Grand Council of Two Hundred. No one knew where he had gone. Lorenzino was gone too, at least he did not make his usual early morning call. All the houses of their mistresses and other boon-companions were searched in vain, but apparently no one dreamt of calling at Lorenzino's, across the way. Probably, it was thought, the two had gone off to Cafogginolo—their favourite haunt.

Madonna Maria, Messer Jacopo de' Salviati's daughter, the widow of Giovanni de' Medici, " delle Bande Nere," who resided near Lorenzino, certainly heard loud cries which terrified her, but it was not an